THE GAY AND LESBIAN
QUOTATION BOOK

The
Gay and Lesbian
Quotation
Book

A Literary Companion

QUENTIN CRISP

ROBERT HALE · LONDON

© *Blue Cliff Editions 1989*
First published in Great Britain 1995 by arrangement
with Macmillan Publishing, Simon & Schuster

ISBN 0 7090 5605 2

Robert Hale Limited
Clerkenwell House
Clerkenwell Green
London EC1R 0HT

The right of Quentin Crisp to be identified as
author of this work has been asserted by him
in accordance with the Copyright, Designs and
Patents Act 1988.

2   4   6   8   10   9   7   5   3   1

*Although most of the quotations in this book deal with homosexuality,
the mention of any person's name does not imply his or her sexual
preference.*

The lines by W.H. Auden from 'Dichtung und Wahrheit' and
'The More Loving One' are used with the permission of Faber &
Faber Ltd, Random House, Inc. and Edward Mendelson, William
Meredith and Monroe K. Spears, Executors of the Estate of W.H.
Auden.

The quotation from Jonathan Katz and from the documents
collected in his books *Gay American History* and *Gay/Lesbian
Almanac* are used with permission.

Grateful acknowledgement is made for permission to reprint from
The Gay Spirit edited by Mark Thompson
(St Martin's Press 1987).

Derek Doyle & Associates, Mold, Clwyd.
Printed and bound in Great Britain by
WBC Book Manufacturers Ltd.

Contents

Introduction

People are neither heterosexual nor homosexual; they are merely sexual.

This has, presumably, been their nature from the beginning of human history, but attitudes towards this unpleasant fact have changed drastically from time to time and from one tribe to another. As in the studies of medicine and of astronomy, so in the matter of being gay, ideas have altered more rapidly in the past century than in all of previous recorded time. I have lived through the last eighty of these years of bewildering change, and in spite of all the terror and all the disillusionment would still maintain that the situation for homosexual men and women has improved.

Perhaps I take this sanguine view because I was born in England, which is such a thin-lipped island, and grew up in the suburbs of London, where it was not known that sex of any kind was here to stay. Beyond those neat front lawns, behind those carefully drawn curtains, it was hoped that if no one mentioned the beastly thing, it would go away. I never heard even the most oblique allusion to any of the more adventurous forms of carnality until I was at least twenty years old. My various oddities of appearance and behaviour were deemed merely to be an irritating method of drawing attention to myself. Had I been born sixty years later and in another country, at least my problem would have been recognized even if it had been greeted with disapproval.

The sexual explosion that has recently burst upon us was caused by the fact that ever since the first Beatle twanged the first note on his guitar, money has fallen into the hands of the young. Until then juveniles were paupers; I can vouch for this statement from experience. As a child I was a dear little thing, a sort of toy for adults to play with, until I reached the age of ten. Then, when this flagrant imposture could not be maintained a moment longer either by me or by my mother, an angry silence reigned until I reluctantly agreed to be classified as a doubtful and doubting adult. I then received the equivalent of 20p. I could not protest; I could not march; I could not buy or ride a motorbike; I could not get drunk or take drugs. I wasn't too good to do any of these things; I was too poor. My parents could see that I was miserable but at least I was quiet.

Now adolescents have money and, therefore, they have power. The world panders to them; there is a teenage market. Before this came into being I do not think that any manufacturer could have predicted what its principal wares would be, but now we know. They are skintight clothes and CDs. These weird products are, of course, only the outward and visible signs of an inward and carnal disgrace. They are the trappings of unbridled sensuality. The young have always wanted more sexual freedom than their parents thought was good for them and have usually cared less about a career than their elders would wish. Now they have their way. Getting on is out; getting off is in.

Inevitably, once sex in general could be mentioned more frequently and more crudely, it was not long before kinky sex also became a subject for contemplation and discussion.

In spite of this, caution should be exercised before assuming that we have entered a permissive society. Fundamentally, there is no such thing. A society is a large group of people who think they have something in common and who know that it is by the recognition and promotion of their homogeneity that they survive. Their communal life depends on the invention of a set of rules that inevitably limits the activities of its members – that name, condemn and even punish those who commit what are in their judgement antisocial acts.

What we now endure is not so much an age of permissiveness as one of outspokenness. This minor revolution has affected our attitude towards sex more conspicuously than towards any other aspect of human behaviour precisely because, until the sixties, it was the subject about which the least was said – in public, anyway.

Viewed in the hideous arc light that became focused upon it, homosexuality appeared at first to be primarily a masculine phenomenon. This was because, until very recently, though women talked more than men, they shouted very much less. It was therefore the conversation of men that was more often heard and more seriously heeded. Women were thought to concern themselves principally with their immediate surroundings, their families and their friends, while men seemed to have few friends and to ignore their families completely; they concentrated upon their relationships with the world.

Historically, lesbian friendships are characterized not only by their longevity but also by a dignity so often lacking in male relationships. The union of Miss Stein and Miss Toklas is a perfect example. Can there ever have been a love so well known and yet so discreet?

In the hope of obtaining what they consider to be their rights, many women have discarded some of the more extreme symbols of femininity. In the minds of some people this has led to a midunderstanding. I have even heard the opinion expressed that lesbianism is a political movement. This idea is, of course, founded on the misconception that all homosexual women are mannish, that they look like Miss Stein or, at the very least, like Radclyffe Hall. This is a mirror image of the notion that all gay men are effeminate. Both these ideas are false, but they are maintained against all evidence to the contrary because they are tidy.

In England, before some of the laws of England condemning all forms of homosexual activity were repealed, a certain amount of market research into the subject was undertaken by the government. Women armed with clipboards went from door to door asking astonished housewives for their opinions about homosexuality. Early in each interview they were asked this question: 'If you were told that you were about to meet a homosexual man, what kind of person would you expect to see?' Almost without exception the reply was, 'Oh, you know. Someone a bit actorish – wearing bright colours and so on.' Later on they were asked if they knew any gay men. If they did, they were asked what these boys looked like. To this query the answer more often than not was 'Just like anybody else.'

The traditional image of homosexual men and women persists only because it makes them easier to recognize and, consequently, easier to control.

With bowed head, I must confess that in my youth I too made the same ridiculous assumptions as the rest of the world. As I strolled about London the only homosexual boys that I saw or, at least, was sure that I saw were what in those days were called the fairies or pansies. From then on I either lived at home in a numbed trance of inertia or in lively misery among those obvious members of my tribe.

If our changing world could be described sexually, I would say it was becoming more masculine. In homosexual terms this means that lesbians – nay, that all women – are becoming more butch and that gay men are moving further and further from their old-fashioned camp appearance and manner. This latter trend has become so marked that in Chicago there are bars that quite shamelessly designate themselves as gay but on the walls of which hang notices warning patrons that the management takes exception to the slightest whiff of cologne or the faintest glint of precious stones. This new form of discrimination is a manifestation of another unalterable law, which states that if one group of people envies another, given the least opportunity, it will imitate the worst characteristics of the species it admires.

Gay men imitate the real world. What else can they imitate? Now that traditional notions of femininity have disappeared from the real world, they have disappeared from the gay world as well. So inevitably, and possibly against its will, the homosexual community apes its environment. It goes beyond eschewing femininity; it shuns anything that might be called finesse.

In a time outworn, homosexual affairs were conducted as though they were quasi-heterosexual. There used to be at least a token wooing, a whirlwind courtship, even a

11

miniscule trace of chivalry lavished on the nymph by the satyr. Now in this inner world, as in the outer one that threatens it, delicacy is dead. Sex is no longer a means by which one human being expresses his interest in or admiration for another. Where once there was a romance, there is now nothing more edifying than that gross pooling of primitive urges that used merely to be the pastime of English public schoolboys.

For a while the epicene landscape in which we now find ourselves seemed to be a haven in which homosexuality could flourish. If heterosexuals were going to admit and even explore the androgynous attributes of their natures, it looked as though there might be at least an uneasy truce between them and the homosexual population – a chance for a tentative movement by society's outcasts towards the heart of the world. I sincerely imagined that the exiles wanted to come home. As I like people and am indifferent to their sex, this trend was especially welcome to me. Alas, it was short-lived; the tide has ebbed.

When I was really young I lived alone, and I was very lonely. And I would go and sit in a café in the hope that the waitress would speak to me. But after a bit you meet people, and through them you meet other people. In fact, up until about the age of twenty-five, most gay men and women are very glad to find others of their tribe at gay clubs. After the age of twenty-five I think you have to say, 'Well, this is my life, and I've got to learn to live it without community.' Those who try to invent a gay community only put themselves at a greater distance from the world. If you sink your individuality into a group identity, you will end up in the same prison that you were in when your mother said, 'Why don't you cut your hair?'

The so uncivil rights movements has put an abrupt end to any hope of minorities being absorbed into the mainstream of humanity. The impatience of the species is at the root of this reversal of fortune. Anger begets anger. It is in the very nature of integration that you cannot fight for it – you can only wait. If you sue for integration, you place yourself in the same position as a suitor who asks, 'Do you really love me?' The answer is almost certain to be an irritable 'OK, I love you. Now will you sit down and shut up?' What good is that?

At first I was shocked by what seemed to me a strategic error on the part of the would-be social reformers, and I was foolish enough to voice my misgivings. I was very soon made reluctantly to realize that if the gay community ever wished to enter the real world, it no longer does so. There is a movement afoot that those who like long words will one day term 'reghettoization'. This is easily recognizable as a subsection of the well-known ideal of being separate but equal. I fear that this goal may be a mirage. As the playwright Donna Severin says, 'If they could just get over their heterophobia, all would be well.'

Thus, in varying degrees, tolerance of homosexuality by the straight world and by gay men and women of one another is offered and withdrawn, accepted and rejected with bewildering rapidity as the decades rush past us.

It seems infinitely worthwhile and even urgent to try to record all these fascinating vicissitudes of relationship, all these shifts of moral emphasis that have disturbed our lives, but how is it best to be done? An abstruse philosophical tome will only ever be read by philosophers. To the average person some less laborious method must be found in which to present this eternal problem. What better way can there be than to compile, in an easily accessible form, the ideas on this subject, of people throughout the ages on both sides of the fence, expressed in their own words?

This is not, however, a joke book, nor is it an anthology of aphorisms – of ugly truths prettily phrased. This may surprise some potential readers who think of epigrams and poetry as the everyday speech of a certain category of gay men. In these pages can be heard both elegant and crude exclamations of disbelief or contempt or sheer panic from the unenlightened. Some of these express a genuine moral indignation; others are only the voice of a society determined to preserve itself at all costs from a force that it considers subversive but that in reality is, at its worst, iconoclastic and, at its least harmful, merely sterile and frivolous. From within the stockade come occasional cries of mourning, darkening growls of rage and, elsewhere, considered opinions from the gay community about its human environment and about itself.

Q.C.

Art and Literature

Those unnatural crimes and vile affections, which are most scandalous at present, and carefully concealed, or most severely punished, were openly avowed among the Greeks and Romans, even in their politest ages; and their most elegant and celebrated poets have defiled their compositions by the mention of such detestable amors, without any expressions of abhorrence, or even of disapprobation; nay, often in a way, which sanctions them, and almost wins the unwary reader to palliate, or even approve them!

THOMAS SCOTT (1423-1500)

Nay, e'en our bard, Dame Nature's darling child,
Felt the strange impulse, and his hours beguiled
In penning sonnets to a stripling's praise,
Such as would damn a poet now-a-days.

ENGLISH POET 1833
on Shakespeare
from *Don Leon*, a purported autobiographical poem of
Byron's life

When you read these, I, that was visible, am become
    invisible,
Now it is you, compact, visible, realizing my poems,
    seeking me,
Fancying how happy you were, if I could be with you,
    and become your lover;
Be it as if I were with you. Be not too certain but I am
    now with you.
WALT WHITMAN (1819-92)

There is no such thing as a moral or an immoral book.
Books are well written, or badly written. That is all.
OSCAR WILDE (1854-1900)

I never travel without my diary. One should always have
something sensational to read in the train.
OSCAR WILDE (1854-1900)
The Importance of Being Earnest

If ever there was a writer whose prayer to posterity might
well have been 'Read my works and let my life alone,' it was
Oscar [Wilde].
GEORGE BERNARD SHAW (1856-1950)

This love is misunderstood and despised, persecuted, and
misinterpreted as nothing else in the world! ... They
murder our love – and it lives. They strangle our cry – and
the future resounds with it! They have murdered my books.
But my books will live ... Another judgment will be spoken
by a brighter and better future. When, no one knows. But
it is the only one I accept.
JOHN HENRY MACKAY (1864-1933)

The homosexual theme is common today in Continental fiction. The English-reading public accepts Gide and Proust with a certain complacent wonder – 'How different from the home life of our own dear Queen.'

ROBERT MORSS LOVETT (1870-1956)

It has always been my belief, or prejudice if you will, that explorations into the field of abnormal sexual psychology were better left to the scientific world and not forced upon the public.

SIDNEY WHIPPLE, 1938

Gentlemen Prefer Gentlemen

ANITA LOOS (1893-1981)
when asked during an interview how she might change the theme of her novel *Gentlemen Prefer Blondes* in view of the changing morals of the sixties.

And I'll stay off Verlaine too; he was always chasing Rimbauds.

DOROTHY PARKER (1893-1967)

In Elizabethan England, where young boys played all the feminine roles on the stage, the device of having a boy playing the romantic role of a girl disguised as a boy fall in love with a man had almost infinite possibilities of amusement for the court and the crowd alike. At other times groups of writers, artists, musicians, and men and women related to the theater have cultivated bisexuality out of a delight with personality, regardless of race or class or sex.

MARGARET MEAD (1901-78)

The Corsican boys, in the late 1930s, were not everyone's cup of tea. *I* find nudes of girls in black stockings singularly unappetizing.

CECIL BEATON (1902-80)
regarding his homoerotic nude portraits of black Moroccan boys

Nobody will believe me, of course, but Diaghilev did not know anything about dancing. His real interest in ballet was sexual. He could not bear the sight of Danilova and would say to me, 'Her tits make me want to vomit.' Once when I was standing next to him at a rehearsal for *Apollo*, he said, 'How beautiful.' I agreed, thinking that he was referring to the music, but he quickly corrected me: 'No, no. I mean Lifar's ass, it is like a rose.'

GEORGE BALANCHINE (1904-83)

[Homosexuals are] indistinguishable from the straight man, except that they have more sensibility and they are more inclined to be good artists.

TENNESSEE WILLIAMS (1912-83)

He [Stephen Crane] now began a novel about a boy prostitute. ... It was going to be called *Flowers of Asphalt* and was to be 'longer than anything he had done.' But Hamlin Garland, when Crane read him some of it, was horrified and begged him to stop ... The manuscript has not been traced.

JOHN BERRYMAN (1914-72)

That naked little man tells the whole fuckin' world you're a big success.
>   ROCK HUDSON (1925-85)
>   on the Oscar

By the end of the year 2000 the whole world will be homosexual!
>   FEDERICO FELLINI
>   shouted by a transvestite at the end of the film *La Dolce Vita*, 1960

[*Victim*] was the first film in which a man said 'I love you' to another man. I wrote that scene in. I said, 'There's no point in half-measures. We either make a film about queers or we don't.'
>   DIRK BOGARDE, 1961

You wouldn't expect me to only make films with gay themes because I am gay?
>   RAINER WERNER FASSBINDER (1946-82)

The list of homosexuals in the theater is long, distinguished and international. It is also self-perpetuating.
>   *The New York Times*, 1963

Arthur Miller is the only major playwright since World War II who had not been associated with homosexuality. He is also the only Jew.
>   WILLIAM GOLDMAN, 1969

If a swamp alligator could talk, it would sound like Tennessee Williams.
>   REX REED, 1972

If you are doing a drama or a comedy or a talk show about homosexuality, you have an obligation to do your homework and free yourself from the myths.

> Gay Activists Alliance and National Gay Task Force, 1973

I won't play lesbians, honey. Not this kid.

> JANE WYMAN, 1976

I didn't want to play a lesbian at that time. Not very many women played recognizable lesbian roles in 1968, and that had a bearing on my decision. Now, of course, I think that the truth is filtering down to all of us, but I still don't think I'd play the part.

> ANGELA LANSBURY, 1976
> comments regarding her decision to turn down the title role in the film *The Killing of Sister George*

Don't play no faggots.

> SYLVESTER STALLONE, 1978
> advice to Perry King, regarding his acceptance of the role of a gay man in the film *A Different Story*

I'm obviously a homosexual writer with hardly a woman in his books.

> WILLIAM S. BURROUGHS, 1978

The Children's Hour by Lillian Hellman was rumored to be a leading contender for the Pulitzer Prize for 1934-35, but it was bypassed, presumably because it dealt with charges of lesbianism ... Its supporters denounced the Pulitzer Committee for cowardice and censorship.

> ABE LAUFE, 1978

Gay people don't need any more screen martyrs.
HOWARD ROSENMAN, 1979

This is not a play about measles.
LARRY KRAMER, 1980s
regarding his play on AIDS, *The Normal Heart*

Isn't it peculiar that in a movie [*La Cage aux Folles*] that celebrates a long-lasting lovers' marriage, we never once see the lovers kiss?
DAVID ANSEN, 1980

Why couldn't this collection be locked up again, at least for several decades? ... Eleanor Roosevelt was a great woman and her effusively affectionate letters should be removed until the year 2000.
DORIS FABER, 1980
spoken to the library director of the National Archives regarding the love letters of Eleanor Roosevelt and Lorena Hickock. The archives ruled against suppression of the letters and Ms Faber grudgingly used them in her biography of Hickock

In Japan in the 1970s, Mishima was deliberately forgotten. But now nationalism is stronger and the gay liberation movement is moving and growing. So Mishima is a cultural hero to many groups, including gay men and right-wing military fans. Also those who love his poetry and literature.
NAGASA OSHIMA, 1984
Japanese film director

He [Little Richard] was like nothing anyone had ever seen. Before 'King of the Blues', he announced himself. 'And the Queen too!' His lyrics to 'Tutti-Frutti' had to be cleaned up

21

before a Hollywood company agreed to record it, but when they were, and they did, he became the King and Queen of Rock 'n' Roll besides.

ANDREW HOLLERAN, 1980s.

A gay poem is one that's sexually attracted to other poems.

WILLIAM BARBER, 1980s

According to this movie [*Personal Best*], lesbianism is just something you catch in the locker room, like athlete's foot.

REX REED, 1982

The gay tradition in poetry is a substantial one, more so in cultures other than the Western. The Greek, Persian, Arabic and Japanese cultures all produced openly homoerotic verse, whereas in Europe, the fervid morbidities of Christianity led to the suppression of gay writing, or at best its concealment by the alteration of gender – a sort of literary sexchange.

IAN YOUNG, 1982

Years ago, when I was editor [of the gay newspaper *The Advocate*], we had planned to drop those nasty classifieds to make the paper more acceptable to large national advertisers and, we thought, to attract more bourgeois subscribers. The slightest bit of market research proved that any such move would have been a disaster.

JOHN PRESTON, 1983

I think gay playwrights should be able to use their truths. A gay playwright can write about gay people and be just as universal as a straight person.

JOHN GLINES, 1983

For homosexuals, [the play *La Cage aux Folles*], even more than *Torch Song Trilogy*, is the Broadway legitimization of their modus vivendi, all the way from respectably bourgeois outrageously transvestite, via a budget of $5 million.

JOHN SIMON, 1983

Critics are forever discovering homosexual references in my plays where they don't exist.

EDWARD ALBEE, 1983

It would be easy to extend the list of gay lives that have been misappropriated and rewritten, from Sappho to Willa Cather, from Socrates to Herman Melville. It is time to reclaim some of these lives.

ROBERT K. MARTIN, 1983

Every year, they publish thousands of non-gay books which they know have no hope of commercial success, and yet they are reluctant to move further into the gay market than to publish Gore Vidal and Truman Capote ... Gay literature is moving into our own hands.

NORMAN LAURILLA, 1984

As for overt homosexuality in pre-1960 films, it was not attempted and not possible. Sonnets have fourteen lines. You wrote sonnets then and there was never an extra or an odd line ... but subtexts did occasionally insert themselves.

GORE VIDAL, 1985

If Michelangelo were a heterosexual, the Sistine Chapel would have been painted basic white and with a roller.

RITA MAE BROWN, 1988

According to Steven [Spielberg], middle America simply would not sit still for me on top and Shug on bottom, so we made it less explicit. This way we won't offend anyone.

    WHOOPI GOLDBERG, 1985

    on the lesbian love scene in *The Color Purple*

Like a gaudy East Indian purse; outrageous in color, embroidered in cliché design, the worth of these plays lies ultimately in the tiny mirrors woven into the fabric wherein we catch our reflections. Perhaps you'll see a little of yourself on the phone with Arnold's 'Why don't you love me anymore?' call.

    HARVEY FIERSTEIN, 1985

Although *All About Eve* is a wonderfully witty movie, do not use any of its lines in life – or in a [gay] bar.

    T.T. WITOMSKI, 1985

Try to calmly accept the fact that Baryshnikov is straight. Don't take an overdose every time you see him photographed with a woman.

    TONY LANG, 1985

Homosexuals have commonly been treated shabbily in detective fiction – vilified, pitied, at best patonized. This was neither fair nor honest. When I sat down to write *Fadeout* in 1967 I wanted to write a good, compelling whodunit, but I also wanted to right some wrongs.

    JOSEPH HANSEN, 1985

Virginia Woolf exemplifies the problem of deciding who is a lesbian writer.

    MARGARET CRUIKSHANK, 1986

I have encountered clients who enter therapy questioning their adequacy as lovers, women, and indeed as lesbians because they find themselves unable to measure up to standards set by the heroines of post-liberation lesbian romantic novels.

LAURA S. BROWN, 1986
American psychologist/sexologist

I've never fully trusted a gay man who doesn't love Judy Garland.

GREGG HOWE, 1986

They're not effeminate either, some of them are really manly and you'd never dream they were queer. Not from the look of them. But I can always tell 'cos they've *all* got LPs of Judy Garland.

JOE ORTON (1933-67)

The opera queen ... is a civic institution, like the cop on the corner. He serves an important function, like that served at the gladiatorial games by Caesar's thumb. No singer who hasn't won her faction among opera queens can be said to have arrived, regardless of how often she's been on the 'Johnny Carson Show'.

IVAN MARTINSON, 1986

One of the rare things about being gay is that you can write about things that weren't discussed before fifty years ago. Only since then, which is a rather short time, have people been in any way open about homosexuality, and there is still a lot more to be discussed.

EDMUND WHITE, 1988

I like the word *gay*, though I think of myself more as *queer*. I believe the strength in my work [as a playwright] comes from that perspective – my being an outsider.

HOLLY HUGHES, 1988

If you want to know who the oppressed minorities in America are, you simply look at who gets their own shelf in the bookstore. A black shelf, a women's shelf, and a gay shelf.

ARMISTEAD MAUPIN, 1988

I think it's largely because of the gay content that my plays are produced.

LANFORD WILSON, 1988

People often ask, was Shakespeare gay? No, he was beyond being gay. He wasn't even bisexual. He was everything with equal passion.

IAN MCKELLAN, 1988

I find that a lot of gay writing today is more specifically directed at gay people. We're under a siege. Gay artists are trying to create a protected place where we can still have some pride.

LANFORD WILSON, 1988

Traditionally men's room walls have been a major outlet for homosexuals to express themselves directly and honestly. The writing on men's room walls is among the finest this country has produced.

BOYD MCDONALD, 1988

Beauty

Lovers look at none of the bodily charms of their favourites more than at their eyes, wherein dwells the secret of boyish virtues.

ARISTOTLE (384 BC-322BC)

See, his beard is sprouting yet
Beauty's fringes delicate;
Delicately through my heart
Passion's thrilling raptures dart.

IBN SARA
Arabian poet

Oh here's to the boy that is pale as snow,
   And to those with the color of honey:
I dote on them dark and I'll have them when tow
   And I love them when open and sunny.

I covet them fair and I don't mind them thin,
   I adore them as brown as a pebble:
But the best of the bunch have a rich olive skin
   And flashing black eyes like the devil.

STRATO, c. AD 2

Come bathe in the scented waters,
  And weave for us garlands bright;
For boys and wine won't stay for ever,
  And the grave offers no delight.
  STRATO, *c.* AD 2

Labienus, each hair on your bosom that grows,
  On your arms, on your legs, with much trouble
You shave, and your belly's appurtenance shows
  Like a newly mown field with its stubble,
Thus blooming and sweet as the breath of the morn,
  Your mistress entwines, you, fond boy,
But you've something behind, neatly shaven and shorn,
  That's scarcely a mistress's toy.
  MARTIAL (40-104)

It is frequently the case with young men [in the monstery] that even when rigorous self-restraint is exercised, the glowing complexion of youth still blossoms forth and becomes a source of desire to those around them. If, therefore, anyone is youthful and physically beautiful, let him keep his attractiveness hidden until his appearance reaches a suitable state.

Sit in a chair far from such a youth; in sleep do not allow your clothing to touch his but, rather, have an old man between you.
  ST BASIL (330?-379?)

Golden haired, fair of face, with a small white neck,
Soft-spoken and gentle – but why do I praise these
    singly?
Everything about you is beautiful and lovely; you have
    no imperfection,

28

Except that such fairness has no business devoting
itself to chastity.
HILARY THE ENGLISHMAN, 1150?

When the young males of our species, brought up together,
feel the force which nature begins to unfold in them, and
fail to find the natural object of their instinct, they fall back
on what resembles it. Often, for two or three years, a young
man resembles a beautiful girl with the freshness of his
complexion, the brilliance of his colouring, and the
sweetness of his eyes; if he is loved, it's because nature
makes a mistake.
VOLTAIRE (1694-1778)

Those who are only aware of beauty in the female sex, and
are hardly or not at all affected by beauty in *our* sex, have
little innate feeling for beauty in art in a general and vital
sense.
JOHANN JOACHIM WINCKELMANN (1717-68)

You are my Greek god, dear youth. I want to sleep with
you, embrace you. When you bathe in Lake Thun, I stare
at your magnificent body with the longing of a girl.
HEINRICH VON KLEIST (1777-1811)

His *voice* first attracted my attention, his *countenance* fixed
it, and his *manners* attached me to him forever.
LORD BYRON (1788-1824)

Winds that breathe about, upon her
(Lines I do not dare)
Whisper, turtle, breathe upon her
That I find her fair.
ANGELINA GRIMKÉ WELD (1805-79)

29

While they discuss I am silent, and go bathe and admire
    myself.
Welcome is every organ and attribute of me, and of any
    man hearty and clean,
Not an inch nor a particle of an inch is vile, and none
    shall be less familiar than the rest.
    WALT WHITMAN (1819-92)

You, proud curve-lipped youth, with brown sensitive
    face,
Why, suddenly, as you sat there on the grass, did you
    turn full upon me those twin black eyes of yours,
With gaze so absorbing, so intense, I a strong man
    trembled and was faint?
    EDWARD CARPENTER (1844-1929)

'But was Narcissus beautiful?' said the pool

'Who should know better than you?' answered the
Oreads.

'Us he did ever pass by, but you he sought for, and would
lie on your banks and look down at you, and in the mirror
of your waters he would mirror his own beauty.'

And the pool answered, 'But I loved Narcissus because,
as he lay on my banks and looked down at me, in the mirror
of his eyes I saw ever my own beauty mirrored.'
    OSCAR WILDE (1854-1900)
    Poems in Prose

It is a marvel that those red rose-leaf lips of yours should
have been made no less for the music of song than for the
madness of kissing.
    OSCAR WILDE (1854-1900)
    from a letter to Lord Alfred Douglas, submitted as
    evidence at his trial for sodomy

My dear, you used to be quite a dish; now you're quite a tureen.
>   SOMERSET MAUGHAM (1874-1965)
>   to his lover, Alan Searle

> WIDOW: I have heard you do not like the fair sex.
> CAPTAIN CONRAD: The fair sex? Which one is that?
>   J.R. ACKERLEY, 1935
>   *The Prisoners of War*

A thing of beauty is a boy forever.
>   CARL VAN VECHTEN (1880-1964)

It's better to be looked over than overlooked.
>   MAE WEST (1892-1980)

I will love you whatever happens, even though you put on twenty pounds or become afflicted with a moustache.
>   W.H. AUDEN (1907-73)

Chekhov was probably gay. But he was very ill, and whether or not he practised his sexual inclination ... if you were to look at early pictures of him you would see that he was a very beautiful man with a very sensitive face that you were not likely to encounter among straight men.
>   TENNESSEE WILLIAMS (1918-83)

[Noel] Coward invented the concept of cool. And if his face suggested an old boot, it was unquestionably hand-made.
>   KENNETH TYNAN (1927-80)

When you think of a bombshell, you think of Monroe or Mansfield, you don't think of a three-hundred-pound man. People like to be shocked.

    DIVINE (1946-88)

At any time you may witness couplings of white with black, beauty with horror, aardvark with dinosaur, panda with pachyderm, skinny-old-slate-gray-potbelly-bald with chubby-old-slate-gray-potbelly-bald, heartbreakingly gentle with stimulatingly rugged – but always, paradoxically, like with like.

    NED ROREM, 1967
    from his description of a New York bathhouse

Although I am not a Lesbian, I do share the normal human response of whatever is attractive physically in either sex.

    GORE VIDAL, 1968
    Myra Breckinridge, in *Myra Breckinridge*

It's the daylight you gotta watch out for. Face it, a thing of beauty is a joy till sunrise.

    HARVEY FIERSTEIN, 1981
    Arnold, in *Torch Song Trilogy*

Gay society, whether one likes it or not, is based very much on looks. A person's physique, not his personality, often attracts the initial response. When men first seek out other men they don't generally inquire, 'Does he have a brilliant mind?' The presentation of one's flesh gets first notice.

    ROY F. WOOD, 1985

Don't augment a tan with anything from a bottle.
TONY LANG, 1985

Don't wear anything made out of old parachutes.
TONY LANG, 1985

Every primer on meeting new friends and winning lovers seems to intone *Be yourself*. I'm not sure that's such good advice. Better to go to a gay bar being the person you want to be.
T.R. WITOMSKI, 1985

Coming Out

I dare not tell it in words – not even in these songs.
WALT WHITMAN (1819-92)

Why do you suppose that Noel [Coward] or I never stuck our personal predilections down the public's throats? Because we know it would outrage them. Believe me, I know what I'm talking about. Don't put your head in a noose.
SOMERSET MAUGHAM (1874-1965)

Indiscretion has always seemed to me one of the privileges of tact.
NATALIE CLIFFORD BARNEY (1876-1972)

Let me tell you something that Mae West said. She was asked about the men she was seen with in public. And she replied, 'It's not the men you see me with, it's the men you don't see me with.' That is true of everybody in public life.
CECIL BEATON (1902-80)

DAVID FROST: Are you a homosexual?
TENNESSEE WILLIAMS: I cover the waterfront.
TENNESSEE WILIAMS (1912-83)

Everybody knew I was a gay playwright. Many, many years ago *Time* was the first publication to spell it out, that I was homosexual. I didn't give a damn.
TENNESSEE WILLIAMS (1912-83)

Perhaps most actors are latent homosexuals and we cover it with drink. I was once a homosexual, but it didn't work.
RICHARD BURTON (1925-84)

I like to keep my secrets to myself, and I guess they will die with me.
ROCK HUDSON (1925-85)

Homosexuality shears across the spectrum of American life – the professions, the arts, business and labor. It always has. But today, especially in big cities, homosexuals are discarding their furtive ways and openly admitting, even flaunting, their deviation.
LIFE MAGAZINE, 1964

Boys-R-Us
T-SHIRT SLOGAN, 1970s

If I look it, I probably am.
T-SHIRT SLOGAN, 1970s

From the beginning of the gay liberation movement, the Stonewall riots of June, 1969, the *Times* and other elements of the mass media have misunderstood just how traumatic and new and courageous is 'coming out'.
STUART BYRON, 1972

I came out of the closet at Columbia in 1946. The first person I told about it was Kerouac, 'cause I was in love with him. He was staying in my room up in the bed, and I was

sleeping on a pallet on the floor. I said, 'Jack, you know, I love you, and I want to sleep with you, and I really like men.' And he said, 'Oooooh, no ...'
ALLEN GINSBERG, 1975

Let the bullets that rip through my brain smash through every closet door in the nation.
HARVEY MILK (1930-78)

Now Allen Ginsberg gets up before an audience of college students and talks about how he jacked off Peter Orlovsky last night, and they all cheer. Forty years ago they'd have been ridden out on a rail. So that is a terrific change.
WILLIAM S. BURROUGHS, 1978

Charles Laughton played every kind of part but never a homosexual. People knew he was gay, but his public image never betrayed his private reality. So he was safe. I wasn't safe.
ROBERT LA TOURNEAUX, 1978

Ever since I had that interview in which I said I was bisexual it seems twice as many people wave at me in the street.
ELTON JOHN, 1980s

Like many men, I too have had homosexual experiences and I am not ashamed.
MARLON BRANDO, 1980s

Most of us have struggled, for a time at least, against the realization of our gayness, and coming out is therefore a long and painful process. I fought my homosexuality for a long time.

DENNIS ALTMAN, 1980s

We don't have one; we don't have a word because we don't have the thing itself. You know, I think the name is the most important aspect of the thing it means. I think what we call 'coming out' for gay people is saying 'I am gay.' Nobody knows that you are gay until you say it – even if you are effeminate or show some outward signs that you are gay. It's not the same for, say, blacks, and the case is clearer here than it is for Jews: nobody will know that you are gay – perhaps not even yourself – unless you say it.

GUY HOCQUENGHEM, 1980s
response to the question, 'What is the word for *gay* in French?'

During the heterosexual years it was rumored that I took on eight men at one time. During the lesbian years, it was rumored that I had orgies in which my daughter (aged eleven, twelve, thirteen) participated. For the full year after I came out, she was ostracized by her peers – only a few friends remained loyal (though remain loyal they did). She, as I, had been branded a pervert and a whore (take your pick).

MARCIA FREEDMAN, 1982

When Oscar Wilde 'feasted with panthers', he was not, as some have suggested, seeking his own destruction; he was testing the limits of his own disguise.

ROBERT K. MARTIN, 1983

37

Speaking for myself, in a way I did not anticipate a decade ago, the self-acceptance and public proclamation of 'gay' has in some ways, in some contexts, made that category less important, less all-defining than it was when they still held it over me and us as an essential dirty secret of the soul.

    JONATHAN KATZ, 1983

No matter how far in or out of the closet you are – you have a next step.

    AD SLOGAN, 1988
    National March on Washington

I feel sad for all of the thousands of women who fantasized about being in his arms, who now have to realize that he never really cared about them. I heard one older woman say, 'I used to dream about him; too bad that he really didn't like erotic relations with women.'

    RUTH WESTHEIMER, 1984
    on Rock Hudson

The Gay closet has many points of discomfort. One is the sheer shame that life must be so secret, that one's citizenship is always dependent on how camouflaged as a heterosexual one appears. The necessary double life means that the Gay person can never simply stand flat-footed on the earth; there are always two people operating in one body, and one of them is a liar.

    JUDITH GRAHN, 1984

When I first came out, nothing scared me more than drag queens.

    DARRELL YATES RIST, 1985

'Coming out' is not an end point in the strategy of adjustment. Rather, it is a conceptual shortcut, an abbreviated way of thinking which fails to encompass the extremely complex process of managing discrediting information about oneself.

MARNY HALL, 1986

Part of the James Dean legend had it that his younger costar [Sal Mineo] 'turned queer' after Dean's untimely death in 1955. According to the story, Sal attempted fruitlessly to contact his fallen friend at a séance. He thereafter wrecked his car in an accident, but fate intervened to spare Sal's life. However, the words 'James Dean' suddenly appeared on the car's windshield, and from that moment on, Sal Mineo was gay.

BOZE HADLEIGH, 1986

There's no need to remain in the closet in Provincetown. The energy that was previously used to build walls of self-protection can be used to create whatever kind of life you like.

RONDO MIECZKOWSKI, 1986

My evocation to gay people is to keep moving beyond the Myth of the Homosexual. Understand that being gay is not the same thing as being homosexual. A new way in gay liberation is forming. In deep and profound ways, none of us has really 'come out' yet.

DON KILHEFNER, 1987

'Coming out' is a deep occasion of the spirit that will not be swayed, of a mind that must know itself through the body. Then at last we're on our way; then we *make* our way.
AARON SHURIN, 1987

Coming out is more than a prescription to a contained lifestyle; it is an ongoing experience of many dimensions.
MARK THOMPSON, 1987

For me there's no closet to go back to. I don't have a thing to do with closets. I don't see how you have the option to run back in once you run out and deal, and I prefer it out so much more.
ESSEX HEMPHILL, 1988

The truth popped out, and in popping out, the millstone was released, and I realized that being in the closet had been a terrible burden.
IAN MCKELLAN, 1988

There's a glorious, ecstatic feeling in being seen, in being out there, especially after so many years of hiding. This is me, come and take it.
SARA CYTRON, 1988

Queers United Against Closets (or QUAC)
American protest organization, 1988

I have no interest in educating my parents, my mother in particular. While most of my friends are either out or waiting for their window of opportunity, I'm keeping Momma from the truth.
JAMES MERRETT, 1988

Whatever your sexuality is, there's nothing to be scared about. I mean, there was a lot of fuss back in the time of Stonewall and gay liberation about people 'coming out'. I was never in any kind of a closet to come out of. It simply didn't occur to me to go into a closet.

DAVID STEVENS, 1988

Anglo gay boys are left much more to their own devices in coming-out matters, but we've all had moments when something deep within us revealed itself quite unexpectedly – if we knew how to look. Hidden somewhere in the depths of my own closet is a childhood scrapbook pasted with neatly colored drawings of the Empress Josephine and England's Princess Margaret. Already at age 8, I was meditating on crowns and robes and the meaning of the word *queen*.

HER IMPERIAL HIGHNESS THE GRAND DUCHESS
TATIANA NEVAHOYDOVA, 1988

Education

By the very fact that we breathe our love into handsome boys we keep them from avarice, increase their enjoyment in work, trouble and dangers, and develop their modesty and self-control.

> XENOPHON (434 BC-355 BC)

I am aware, sir, that Plato, in his Symposium, discourseth very eloquently touching the Uranian and Pandemian Venus: but you must remember that in our Universities, Plato is held to be little better than a misleader of youth.

> THOMAS LOVE PEACOCK (1785-1866)
> Dr Folliott, in *Crochet Castle*

At school, friendship is a passion. It entrances the being, it tears the soul. All loves of after-life can never bring its rapture, or its wretchedness; no bliss so absorbing, no pangs of jealousy or despair so crushing and so keen! What tenderness and what devotion; what illimitable confidence; infinite revelations of inmost thoughts; what ecstatic present and romantic future; what bitter estrangements and what melting reconciliations; what scenes of wild recrimination, agitating explanations, passionate correspondence; what insane sensitiveness, and what frantic sensibility; what earthquakes of the heart and whirlwinds of the soul are confined in that simple phrase, a schoolboy's friendship!

BENJAMIN DISRAELI (1804-81)

The talk in the dormitories and studies was of the grossest character, with repulsive scenes of onanism, mutual masturbation and obscene orgies of naked boys in bed together.

JOHN ADDINGTON SYMONDS (1840-93)
from his account of Harrow School, 1852

It is probable that the superior Urnings [gay people] will become, in affairs of the heart, to a large extent the teachers of the future society; and if that is so that their influence will tend to the realization and expression of an attachment less exclusively sensual than the average of today and to the diffusion of this in all directions.

EDWARD CARPENTER (1844-1929)

Oxford is the capital of Romance ... in its own way as memorable as Athens and to me it was even more entrancing.

OSCAR WILDE (1854-1900)

[Clive] educated Maurice, or rather his spirit educated Maurice's spirit, for they themselves became equal. Neither thought 'Am I led; am I leading?' Love had caught him out of triviality and Maurice out of bewilderment in order that two imperfect souls might touch perfection.

E.M. FORSTER (1879-1970)
Narrator, in *Maurice*

The theater will be my medium to sex education. I pride myself on the fact that I have always been ahead of public teachers. I realized the importance of the problem and devoted my career in the theater to the education of the masses. I shall boldly continue to do so, in spite of criticism, insults, and narrow-minded bigots. I believe that when I have my own theater, as I hope to some time in the future, my purpose can go unhindered by silly and old-fashioned taboos and busy bodies.

    MAE WEST (1892-1980)

    two years after the closing of her play *The Drag*, a
    controversial portrait of homosexuals

I hadn't been in prep school more than a month, and I'd slept with all the boys and half the faculty ... Of course, I'm speaking rhetorically!

    TRUMAN CAPORE (1924-84)

'Wasn't it easy being a school-teacher?' I said. 'Oh, it was,' he said, 'it was terrible. And the boys, you know, are such terrible tarts. Once one of them called me into the music room and we sat down and he kissed me, and I mean, what can one do? I didn't dare respond. So I simply smiled and pushed the boy off, with instruction to continue the five-finger exercise.'

    JOE ORTON (1933-67)

Did you hear about the transvestite at Harvard that wanted to spend his junior year abroad?

    AMERICAN JOKE, 1970s

We have no stake in education which is racist, male-chauvinist, anti-working class and antihomosexual. The schools are not people's schools and therefore do not serve the people. They certainly do not serve us as homosexuals, but teach ideology that is destructive to us and helps to keep us social outcasts. What child would have disdain for homosexuals? They have to be taught that.

CHICAGO GAY LIBERATION FOR THE REVOLUTIONARY
PEOPLE'S CONSTITUTIONAL CONVENTION
working paper, 1970

I have often thought that a solution for the ills of the world would be to send all boys to a school that taught them to love one another … I mean get them all into bed together to learn the ecstatic habit of male love.

JAMES BROUGHTON, 1982

By the persistent use of the term *homophile* (instead of the hetero designate gemixtepickle *homosexual*) we educated American public opinion to perceive us no longer as merely perverse performers of criminal acts but as *persons* of a distinct sociopolitical minority.

HARRY HAY, 1987

My anger is, that the government failed to educate us.

BILLY DENVER DONALD
American administrator for the handicapped, 1987
quote embroidered on the quilt panel commemorating his death from AIDS

45

This amendment should go down into the sewer from whence it came.

LOWELL WEICKER, 1988
regarding a Senate proposal permitting religious colleges in Washington, DC, to deny facilities to gay student groups

In Utah, teachers are not allowed to talk about same-sex intercourse as a method of transmission. In Florida, state law requires that parents write permission notes before their children can be told about AIDS. And in countless other school districts around the country, controversial subject matter is simply ignored.

ROBERT W. PETERSON, 1988

All persons, regardless of sexual orientation, should be afforded equal opportunity within the public education system.

NATIONAL EDUCATION ASSOCIATION, 1988

I don't think it's my job to educate people on safe sex. Do I have to wear a condom in my scenes on the screen? This is an R-rated film. This is the '80s. There is AIDS. There is alcoholism. People should be able to figure it out for themselves.

TOM CRUISE, 1988

Employment and Money

Many men ... have spent a talent for a male lover or 300 drachmas for a jar of caviar from the Black Sea.
POLYBIUS (205? BC-125? BC)

For all their faults and their annoying ways
With darling Ganymedes I'd pass my days,
Rather than lead a sumptuous tinselled life
With twenty million dollars and a wife.
MARTIAL (40-104)

The fragrance of profit is pleasing; no one avoids gain.
Wealth, if I should speak plainly, does have a certain
appeal. Anyone who wishes to grow rich is willing to
play this game:
If a man desires boys, he is willing to reward them.
MEDIEVAL MONK, 1120?
Ganymede and Helen

Though a lord may promise much,
And abject poverty constrain me …
I am not one of those inclined to do
What is profitable rather than proper …
I prefer to remain poor and pure
Than to live wealthy and debauched.
    MEDIEVAL MONK, 1200?
    Carmina Burana

JUPITER: Come, gentle Ganymede, and play with me:
    I love thee well, say Juno what she will …
GANYMEDE: I would have a jewel for mine ear,
    And a fine brooch to put in my hat,
And then I'll hug with you an hundred times.
    CHRISTOPHER MARLOW (1564-93)
    Dido, Queen of Carthage

There now ye sit, and with mixt souls embrace,
Gazing upon great *Love's* mysterious Face,
And pity this base world where *Friendship's* made
A bait for sin, or else at best a *Trade*.
    ABRAHAM COWLEY (1618-67)
    David and Jonathan

This practice [homosexuality] took away not only our own
living, but something from all womankind which nature
intended them to have.
    JOHN CLELAND (1709-89)
    Fanny Hill, in *Memoirs of Fanny Hill*

THE CUPBEARER SPEAKS
Prithee leave me, crafty hussy,
    Take thy ringlets brown away:
To my master suits my waiting
    And his kisses are my pay.
Therefore thou, I'm free to wager,
    Hast no love on me to spend:
And thy cheeks, thy breasts, would only
    Be fatiguing to my friend.
JOHANN WOLFGANG VON GOETHE (1749-1832)

Everywhere a new motive of life dawns.
With the liberation of Love, and with it of Sex, with the
sense that these are things – and the joy of them – not to
be dreaded or barred, but to be made use of, wisely and
freely, as a man makes use of his most honored
possession,
Comes a new gladness:
The liberation of a Motive greater than Money,
And the only motive perhaps that can finally take
precedence of Money.
EDWARD CARPENTER (1844-1929)
A Mightier than Mammon

One could never pay too high a price for any sensation.
OSCAR WILDE (1854-1900)

C.F. GILL, prosecutor at Wilde's second trial: You
made handsome presents to all these young fellows?
OSCAR WILDE: Pardon me, I differ. I gave two or three
of them a cigarette case. Boys of that class smoke a
good deal of cigarettes. I have a weakness for
presenting my acquaintances with cigarette cases.

GILL: Rather an expensive habit if indulged in
   indiscriminately, isn't it?
WILDE: Less extravagant than giving jewelled garters to
   ladies.
   OSCAR WILDE (1854-1900)

The bringing up of boys by male persons (slaves in the
ancient times) seems to favour homosexuality; the
frequency of inversion in the present-day nobility is
probably explained by their employment of male servants,
and by the scant care that mothers of that class give to their
children.
   SIGMUND FREUD (1856-1939)

Many of our famous lawyers, doctors, bankers and judges
are homosexualists. Thousands of others suffer because they
are starving for love both in body and soul, and they
become mental prostitutes.
   MAE WEST (1892-1980)

I have some lady impersonators in the play [*Pleasure Man*].
In fact I have five of them. But what of it? If they are going
to close up the play and prevent these people from making a
living because they take the part of female impersonators,
then they should stop other female impersonators from
appearing on the Keith Circuit ... How many thousand
female impersonators do you think there are in the country?
Are they going to put them all out of business?
   MAE WEST (1892-1980)

The instinct of acquisitiveness has more perverts, I believe,
than the instinct of sex ... People seem to me odder about
money than about even their amours. Such amazing

meannesses as one's always coming across, particularly among the rich.

ALDOUS HUXLEY (1894-1963)

It was very much easier for us because we were in the arts. We were never employed by anybody who demanded any kind of concealment, and we were largely on our own – not pleasing any boss, as it were, except ourselves, and that made it easier.

CHRISTOPHER ISHERWOOD (1904-86)

Just being gay really keeps you busy from morn until eve if you do it whole-heartedly ... if you're constantly working for your gay brothers and sisters.

CHRISTOPHER ISHERWOOD (1904-86)

The sexual friendship of two young men, or young girls, follows the lines of economic cleavage when marriage is too expensive or the penalty of illicit intercourse too dear.

T.H. EVANS, 1906

I was not attracted sexually to the old men whom I robbed; what attracted me was their money; so the question was to take their money by beating them or by making them come; the goal was money.

JEAN GENET (1910-86)

I've been turned down for everything, including the WACs.

TRUMAN CAPOTE (1924-84)
on his rejection from the draft

Gay Buy Gay.
>HARVEY MILK (1930-78)
>motto encouraging gay patronage of gay businesses,
>inspired by Harvey Milk's slogan 'Gay for Gay'

Transsexuals who continue to work in the same field after surgery often must sacrifice the status and salary they have earned, reentering the field on a lower level than formerly, under a new name.
>HARRIET SLAVITZ, 1960s

Inverts [homosexuals] are to be found in every conceivable line of work from truck driving to coupon clipping. But they are most concentrated – or most noticeable – in the fields of the creative and performing arts and industries serving women's beauty and fashion needs.
>*The New York Times*, 1963

Homosexuals as well as heterosexuals have emotional hangups. Though that usually comes to an abrupt end – when the boy asks for more money.
>GORE VIDAL, 1969

The jobs into which we are tracked are often low-paying and certainly alienating. And the higher federal income taxation of 'single' people – that is, those whose relationships are not recognized as legal – discriminates against us economically.
>CHICACO GAY LIBERATION FOR THE REVOLUTIONARY
>PEOPLE'S CONSTITUTIONAL CONVENTION
>*working paper*, 1970

[Truman Capote] thinks he's a very rich Society Lady, and spends a great deal of money.
GORE VIDAL, 1973

There is a manneristic fairydom that depends on money, chic, privilege and exclusive, monopolistic high style, and I would say that it is usually accompanied by bitchiness and bad manners and faithless love, too. I like homosexuality where the lovers are friends all their lives, and there are many lovers and many friends.
ALLEN GINSBERG, 1975

I have some good news and some bad news. I just found out my son is a homosexual.
What's the good news?
He's dating a doctor.
JOKE, 1980s

Yes, you know *gay*,
but I need to teach you *queer*
I need to tell you about hostile glares
and false arrests
and you have no defense
a queer can't bear witness
against a lying cop. They call your boss,
you lose your job, there's no redress.
MARTHA SHELLEY, 1982

As for jeans, cowboy shirts and work boots, they at least have the virtue of being cheap. The uniform conceals the rise of what strikes me as a whole new class of gay indigents. Sometimes I have the impression every fourth man on

Christopher Street is out of work, but the poverty is hidden by the costume. Whether this appalling situation should be disguised is another question altogether; is it somehow egalitarian to have both the rich and the poor dressed up as Paul Bunyan?

EDMUND WHITE, 1983

Heterosexuals are not presumed to be sexually irresponsible when they are interviewed for a job, nor are they required to promise chastity. Why should homosexuals be discriminated against in this regard when they seek employment? ... If it be such a criterion, it should apply to heterosexual as well as homosexual people ... I urge him [Mayor Koch] to stand strong against the use of public funds in agencies where equal rights are denied.

PAUL MOORE JR, EPISCOPAL BISHOP OF NEW YORK
letter to *The New York Times*, 1984

Large corporations have never been particularly congenial settings for workers who have diverged from the norms of white, heterosexual, male society. A lesbian who works in such a setting has to face two levels of devaluation: her femaleness and her lesbianism. If she is not white and Anglo-Saxon, she adds a third.

MARNY HALL, 1986

We value differences at Apple. As we prepare for the future, we must remember that diversity in the workplace adds richness.

DEBBIE BIONDOLILLO
Personnel director, Apple Computer, Inc.
regarding the corporation's written ban on
discrimination against gay people

AZT. Whatever you may think of its use as a drug, it was the first ever to be denied to people on the basis of cost factor alone.

SIMON WATNEY, 1988

I will not live with a discharge that says I'm honorable but unfit to serve my country.

MIRIAM BEN-SHALOM, 1988

regarding her legal dispute with the US Army Reserve to re-enlist her after she was discharged for being gay (she won)

There are policemen, schoolteachers, farmers, doctors, playwrights, ministers, chefs, lawyers, artists and politicians. There is a quilt panel for the hairdresser who styled Joan Mondale's hair during the 1984 Democratic Convention, and there is one for the respiratory therapist who tended Ronald Reagan after the 1981 assassination attempt. There are sons and daughters, mothers and fathers, lovers, brothers, friends and grandparents.

CINDY RUSKIN, 1988

on people commemorated on the quilt

Gayness

lest is the man who loves and after early play
  Whereby his limbs are supple made and strong,
  Retiring to his house, with wine and song
 oys with a fair boy on his breast the livelong day!
    SOLON (638? BC-558? BC)

jolden-haired love strikes me again
'ith a purple ball, and calls on me to play
'ith a motley-sandled girl. But she,
ɔr she comes from well-built Lesbos,
nds fault with my hair, for it is white,
nd gapes after another girl.
    ANACREON (572? BC-488? BC)

ɔse who love men and rejoice to lie with and be
ɔraced by men are also the finest boys and young men,
ıg naturally the most manly. The people who accuse
m of shamelessness lie; they do this not from
melessness but from courage, manliness, and virility,
ɔracing what is like them. A clear proof of this is the fact

that as adults they alone acquit themselves as men in public careers.

> ARISTOPHANES (450? BC-385? BC)

Give me a boy whose tender-skin
Owes its fresh bloom to youth, not art;
And for his sake may no girl win
A place in my heart.

> MARTIAL, 40-104

Indeed ... there is some danger that womankind will become unnecessary in the future, with young men instead fulfilling all the needs women used to.

> ST JOHN CHRYSOSTOM (347-407)

What can there be of as much value as a boy faithful to his lover?

> MARBOD, BISHOP OF RENNES (1060?-1123)

While I was still a schoolboy, the charm of my friends greatly captivated me, so that among the foibles and failings with which that age is fraught, my mind surrendered itself completely to emotion and devoted itself to love.

> ST AELRED OF RIEVAULX (1109?-66)

'Disparity divides things: it is rather like things that are
    rightly joined together;
For a man to be linked to a man is a more elegant
    coupling.
In case you had not noticed, there are certain rules of
    grammar

By which articles of the same gender must be coupled
    together.'
MEDIEVAL POET, 1120?
Ganymede, in *Ganymede and Helen*

Many the girls and women I have loved, both lad and man;
many the boys and men I have loved, both lad and man.
    GERMAN MONK, 1150?

Many you will find for whom the boyish sin is execrable
    in words
But who do not dislike the deed.
The more they detest it with their words – to hide what
    they love and freely do –
The more they indulge it in their acts.
    MEDIEVAL MONK, 1150?

The indiscriminate Venus grasps at any remedy,
But the wise one rejoices with the tender Ganymede.

I have heard it said that he plays Venus more than she,
But Venus is happy, since he only does boys.

Nothing is more certain than this, that Venus would
Be devoid of every sweetness if she lacked Ganymede.

For his face smiles, his complexion shines, his legs are
    soft,
His lap is sweet, his heart gentle and his beauty
    charming;
His demeanor is open, suppressing shyness, his spirit
Is ready for the boyish sin, and his body prepared
To undergo anything his seducer should ask:

This boy surpasses all treasure; nothing is more blessed
than he.
MEDIEVAL MONK, 1150?

The love of which I speak aspires on high;
Woman is too unlike and little does it agree
With a wise and manly heart to burn for her.
The one draws up to heaven, the other down to earth,
The one inhabits the soul, the other the senses.
MICHELANGELO BUONARROTI (1475-1564)

All they that love not tobacco and boys are fools.
CHRISTOPHER MARLOWE (1664-93)

Two loves I have of comfort and despair
Which like two spirits do suggest me still,
The better angel is a man right fair,
The worser spirit a woman coloured ill.
WILLIAM SHAKESPEARE (1564-1616)

Farewell, woman! I intend
Henceforth every night to sit
With my lewd, well-natured friend,
Drinking to engender wit.

Then give me health, wealth, mirth, and wine,
And, if busy love entrenches,
There's a sweet, soft page of mine
Does the trick worth forty wenches.
JOHN WILMOT, EARL OF ROCHESTER (1648-80)

Englishmen were dolts and nidwits not to realize that there
was better sport than with women.
ROBERT HARLEY, EARL OF OXFORD (1661-1724)

How did it come about that a vice which would destroy mankind if it were general, that a sordid outrage against nature, is still so natural?

VOLTAIRE (1694-1778)

Women are kept for nothing but the breed;
For pleasure we must have a Ganymede,
A fine, fresh Hylas, a delicious boy,
To serve our purposes of beastly joy.

CHARLES CHURCHILL (1731-64)

The Greeks knew the difference between love and friendship as well as we – they had distinct terms to signify them by: it seems reasonable therefore to suppose that when they say love they mean love, and that when they say friendship only they mean friendship only.

JEREMY BENTHAM (1748-1832)

We two boys together clinging,
One the other never leaving,
Up and down the roads going, North and South
    excursions making,
Power enjoying, elbows stretching, fingers clutching,
Arm'd and fearless, eating, drinking, sleeping, loving,
No law less than ourselves owning, sailing, soldiering,
    thieving, threatening,
Misers, menials, priests alarming, air breathing, water
    drinking, on the turf or the sea-bench dancing,
Cities wrenching, ease scorning, statutes mocking,
    feebleness chasing,
Fulfilling our foray.

WALT WHITMAN (1819-92)

Pederasty is a disease with which all men are stricken at a certain age.

GUSTAVE FLAUBERT (1821-80)

> EDWARD CARSON, prosecutor at Wilde's trial: What enjoyment was it to you to entertain grooms and coachmen?
>
> OSCAR WILDE: The pleasure to me was being with those who are young, bright, happy, careless, and free. I do not like the sensible and I do not like the old.
>
> OSCAR WILDE (1854-1900)
> from the transcript of his first trial

I would sooner have fifty unnatural vices than one unnatural virtue.

OSCAR WILDE (1854-1900)

The natural attraction between young men & young women is pretty sure to be stronger than this unnatural & fantastic one between girl & girl; but it [the former] can't go to such lengths among respectable young people.

ALICE STONE BLACKWELL, 1882

All men are capable of homosexual object selection and actually accomplish this in the unconscious.

SIGMUND FREUD (1856-1939)

Some of the most prominent men known have been inverts [homosexuals] and perhaps absolute inverts.

SIGMUND FREUD (1856-1939)

I tried to persuade myself that I was three-quarters normal and that only a quarter of me was queer – whereas really it was the other way round.

SOMERSET MAUGHAM (1874-1965)

Went out last night,
With a crowd of my friends,
They must be womens
Cause I don't like mens.

MA RAINEY (1886-1939)

The anomaly [gay love] has been in existence as long as man has. It has been called by many names, some opprobrious, some laudatory. Now that the world dares say sex and sexuality aloud, it seems to be agreed that such individuals shall be called homosexuals, though they, if one may judge from their writings on the subject, prefer to be called 'the intermediate sex'.

JOSEPH COLLINS (1866-1950)

Genuine homosexuality is not a vice, it is an endowment.

JOSEPH COLLINS (1866-1950)

Maids, not to you my mind doth change;
Men I defy, allure, estrange,
Prostrate, make bond or free:
Soft as the stream beneath the plane
To you I sing my love's refrain;
Between us is no thought of pain,
    Peril satiety.

EDITH EMMA COOPER (1862-1914) AND KATHERINE
HARRIS BRADLEY (1846-1914)

I find pleasure in watching women in each other's arms, waltzing well.

GABRIELLE SIDONIE COLETTE (1873-1954)

She [the character Helen Furr] told many then the way of being gay, she taught very many then little ways they could use in being gay. She was living very well, she was gay then, she went on living then, she was regular in being gay, she always was living very well and was gay very well and was telling about little ways one could be learning to use in being gay, and later was telling them quite often, telling them again and again.

GERTRUDE STEIN (1874-1946)
Miss Furr and Miss Skeene

Happiest of all, surely, are those Uranians, ever numerous, who have no wish nor need to fly society – or themselves. Knowing what they are, understanding the natural, moral strength of their position as homosexuals; sure of right on their side, even if it be never accorded to them in the lands where they must live; fortunate in either due self-control or private freedom – day by day, they go through their lives, self-respecting and respected, in relative peace.

EDWARD STEVENSON, 1908

I don't know what I am; no one's ever told me that I'm different and yet I know that I'm different – that's why, I suppose, you've felt as you have done. And for that I forgive you, though whatever it is, it was you and my father who made this body – but what I will never forgive is your daring to try and make me ashamed of my love. I'm not ashamed of it, there's no shame in me.

RADCLYFFE HALL (1886-1943)
Stephen Gordon, in *The Well of Loneliness*

Lesbian love as the designation of love relationships between women is widely used and its meaning is universally understood, at least by all persons at all versed in sexual science. Yet the standard dictionaries which list medical terms ... take no notice of the terms relating to sexual inversion in women.

DOUGLAS C. MCMURTRIE (1888-1944)

Chicago has not developed a euphemism yet for these male perverts. In New York they are known as 'fairies' and wear a red necktie (inverts are generally said to prefer green). In Philadelphia they are known as 'Brownies'.

JAMES G. KIERNAN, 1916

Homosexuality then is love for members of the same sex. It begins at home among brothers and brothers, sisters and sisters, and has always united mothers and daughters, fathers and sons, in bonds of friendly love.

CONSTANCE LONG, 1919

Many people fail to recognize homosexuality when they see it.

LA FOREST POTTER, 1933

Oh, Mr Maugham, but this is a fairyland!

EDNA ST VINCENT MILLAY (1892-1950)
admiring the view from Somerset Maugham's villa in the Mediterranean, known as a gathering place for distinguished gay artists of the day

Come all ye Revelers! – Dance the night unto dawn –
come when you like, with whom you like – wear what
you like – Unconventional? Oh, to be sure – only do be
discreet!

    poster advertising gay dance, the Greenwich Village
Ball, 1930

When you see two women walking hand in hand,
    Just look 'em over and try to understand:
They'll go to those parties – have the lights down low –
    Only those parties where women can go.
BESSIE SMITH (1894-1937)
'The Boy in the Boat'

Ten percent of all men are more or less exclusively
homosexual for at least three years between the ages of 16
and 55.

    ALFRED KINSEY (1894-1956)

Ah, yes, that word [*gay*]. Well, it belonged to another
time. Even if it didn't have the homosexual connotation, it
would hardly be an adjective in popular usage nowadays.
It's rather quaint. Perhaps a word like 'homoerotic' – but
they always object to the prefix 'homo', except in Homo
sapiens, and if it isn't one group that's objecting, it's
another.

    GEORGE CUKOR (1899-1983)

Isn't it curious that female homosexuals want a separate
word for themselves, but there are no separate adjectives or
nouns for female and male heterosexuals?

    GEORGE CUKOR (1899-1983)

We stand in the middle of an uncharted, uninhabited country. That there have been other unions like ours is obvious, but we are unable to draw on their experience. We must create everything for ourselves. And creation is never easy.

> FRANCIS OTTO MATTHIESSEN (1902-50)
> from a letter to his lover, Russell Cheney

Homosexuality is more acceptable, only because blatant heterosexuality is more acceptable.

> CECIL BEATON (1902-80)

I don't feel personally that I'm constantly a part of the gay community; rather a large majority of the people who come to this house happen to be gay.

> CHRISTOPHER ISHERWOOD (1904-86)

One is not born homosexual or normal; each person becomes one or the other according to the accidents in his life and his own reaction to these accidents.

> JEAN-PAUL SARTRE (1905-80)

It is not only a man who can be dangerous to a woman ... In some cases it can be another woman.

> EDOUARD BOURDET, 1926
> D'Aiguines, in *The Captive*

I don't have any theory about homosexuality. I don't even have a theory about undifferentiated desire. I ascertain that I'm homosexual. OK. That's no cause for alarm. How and why are idle questions.

> JEAN GENET (1910-86)

Man alone satisfies man.
JEAN GENET (1910-86)

The time has come, I think, when we must recognize bisexuality as a normal form of human behavior.
MARGARET MEAD (1901-78)

We're saying this whole marvelous thing of being gay, of being a fairy, is much more than just the beautiful part of our sexuality. There is more to be explored and discovered. We're calling on gay people to come out and fly. This is what we think the movement of the age is.
HARRY HAY, 1950

It is not uncommon for lesbians to establish friendly relations with male homosexuals. One reason is that the relationship is apt to be a platonic one and consequently they have no need to fear being seduced, particularly if they harbor antipathy toward men in general.
FRANK CAPRIO, 1954

We have to not only affirm ourselves as an identity, but as a creative force.
MICHAEL FOUCAULT (1926-84)

My mother made me a homosexual.
   If I gave her some yarn, would she make me one too?
   Graffito, 1960s

The very idea of changing to heterosexuality ... is a tacit acknowledgement of inferiority.
FRANK KAMENY
founder of Washington Mattachine Society, 1965

[Horatio] Alger appeared to be living a kind of existence which was homosexual in nature, if not in fact. He had renounced women and the conventional patterns of sex. As far as anyone knows, he had no women friends. All his time was spent either with [Charles] O'Connor [superintendent of the Children's Aid Society Lodging House] or the young boys who surrounded them.

JOHN TEBBEL, 1965

A woman lover is always persistent.

HEDY LAMARR, 1966

All over the United States there are young gay people who think they're going to fail *because* they're gay. I want to show them they can succeed – that they can have hope.

HARVEY MILK (1930-78)

Our tragedy does not derive from our fantasy of what homosexuals are but from our fantasy of what America is. We have made each other up.

ELDRIDGE CLEAVER, 1968
Beverly Axelrod, in *Soul on Ice*

I am going to use the slang term 'gay' as a synonym for homosexual, though I by no means wish to imply by this use that homosexual life is gay in the more traditional sense of the word.

MARTIN HOFFMAN, 1968

There once was a gay chap named Bloom,
Who invited a gent to his room.
They argued all night
As to who had the right
To do what with which and to whom.
LIMERICK, 1970s

Did you hear about the young man who moved to Greenwich Village and turned prematurely gay?
JOKE, 1970s

Gay is a process of attaining mutual and equal social and sensual relationships among all human beings, which is realized only through participation in the free dynamic expression of love among people of the same sex.
GAY REVOLUTION PARTY MANIFESTO, 1970

Sappho Was a Right-On Woman
SIDNEY ABBOTT AND BARBARA LOVE, 1972
title of their book about lesbianism and society

How, by the way, is one to make a noun out of that idiotic adjective *gay?* A *gayist?* A *sprite? Pollyanna?*
GORE VIDAL, 1977

I think that people who are gay verge on being angels, or wayward angels. Gayness is a gift.
HIBISCUS, 1980s

Proust teaches us that every man is homosexual and every woman a lesbian.
CHARLES LUDLAM, 1980s

How may straight San Franciscans does it take to change a light bulb?
Both of them.
    JOKE, 1980s

That I'm homosexual seems like a sure thing – I've associated with myself for nearly forty years.
    MUTSUO TAKAHASHI, 1982

To be gay is to be overwhelmed with the attitudes of other people, and in order to free ourselves from that we have to put those aside and develop our own sense of what is right.
    REVD HARRY BRITT, 1982

Gay lives cannot be examined through straight spectacles.
    ROBERT K. MARTIN, 1983

Ah, everything is lesbian which loves itself
I am lesbian when I really look in the mirror.
    MARTHA COURTOT, 1984

Everyone is basically gay. It's a question of whether they're, you know, willing.
    BOYD MCDONALD, 1985

I would define gay people as possessing a *luminous* quality of being, a differentness that accentuates the gifts of compassion, empathy, healing, interpretation and ena-bling. I see gay people as the *inbetween ones*; those who can entertain irreconcilable differences, who are capable of uniting opposing forces as one; bridge builders who intuit the light and dark of all things.
    MARK THOMPSON, 1987

Gay men have a unique potential within them to experience nature and other beings not as 'objects' to be manipulated and mastered, but as 'subjects', like themselves, to be respected and cherished.

DON KILHEFNER, 1987

Gaiety is a great moral good and a high spiritual value, as well as being a key to the universe.

JAMES BROUGHTON, 1987

It was not, and is not now, in our natures and never part of our dream, to want to conquer nature ... we were always the shy kids who walked with clouds and talked to trees and butterflies.

HARRY HAY, 1987

One of the most insidious concepts used to develop our subculture has been that of *pride*. Because of the relentless nature of our oppression, gay people have had to seize upon the concept of pride in order to measure self-worth. Instilling a *sense* of pride is a justifiable component of any community, but a fixation on pride leads to isolation, inflation of individual egos and greed.

MARK THOMPSON, 1987

I don't want to think about being gay all the time. I want to have my life, my lover, my friends, and I don't want to have to spend my time being scared and angry.

HOWARD CRUSE, 1988

Nebuchadnezzar was a homosexual. He would cast lots every night as to which king, whom he had captured in battle, turn it was for pederasty.

RABBI SHOLOM KLASS, 1988

71

The gay community encompasses people from all walks of life, all economic ranks and all political philosophies.

DELL RICHARDS, 1988

Homosexuality is God's way of insuring that the truly gifted aren't burdened with children.

SAM AUSTIN, 1988

Gender

Men ... show their masculinity throughout their boyhood by the way they make friends with men, and the delight they take in lying beside them and being taken in their arms. And these are the most hopeful of the nation's youth, for theirs is the most virile constitution.
PLATO (427? BC-347 BC)

[Caesar is] every man's wife and every woman's husband.
CURIO THE ELDER, 53 BC

Hail, Queen of Bithynia!
ROMAN SENATE, 49 BC
shouted in the senate upon the arrival of Julius Caesar, recalling his controversial affair with King Nicomedes of Bithynia

When nature formed you, she doubted for a moment
Whether to offer you as a girl or a boy,
But while she sets her mind's eye to settling this,
Behold! You come forth, born as a vision for all.
HILARY THE ENGLISHMAN, 1150?

Some swore he was a maid in man's attire,
For in his looks were all that men desire ...
His dangling tresses that were never shorn,
Had then been cut, and unto Colchos borne,
Would have allured the venus youth of Greece
To hazard more than for the Golden Fleece.
CHRISTOPHER MARLOWE (1564-93)

All men and women woo me. There is a fragrance in their breath.
HENRY DAVID THOREAU (1817-62)

What a good man she was, and what a kind woman.
IVAN TURGENEV (1818-83)
on the death of George Sand in a letter to his friend, Gustave Flaubert

Madame Bovary is me.
GUSTAVE FLAUBERT (1821-80)

If a severe distinction of elements were always maintained the two sexes would soon drift into far latitudes and absolutely cease to understand each other.
EDWARD CARPENTER (1844-1929)

All women become like their mothers. That is their tragedy. No man does. That's his.
OSCAR WILDE (1854-1900)
The Importance of Being Earnest

The belief that a male homosexual is necessarily a misogynist and shuns or despises women has little foundation in fact. In a measure the contrary is true ...

Women find him understanding, intuitive, sympathetic and are thus led into close friendship with him and what might be called spurious intimacy.
JOSEPH COLLINS (1866-1950)

It takes all sorts to make a sex.
SAKI (1870-1916)

What is sauce for the goose may be sauce for the gander, but is not necessarily sauce for the chicken, the duck, the turkey or the guinea hen.
ALICE B. TOKLAS (1877-1967)

The trumpeters, ranging themselves side by side in order, blow one terrific blast:–
'THE TRUTH!!'
at which Orlando woke.
He stretched himself. He rose. He stood upright in complete nakedness before us, and while the trumpets pealed Truth! Truth! Truth! we have no choice left but confess – he was a woman.
VIRGINIA WOOOLF (1882-1941)
Orlando

There is more difference within the sexes than between them.
IVY COMPTON-BURNETT (1892-1969)

In this sable performance of sexual perversion [a drag dance] all of these men are lasciviously dressed in womanly attire, short sleeves, low-necked dresses and the usual ballroom decorations and ornaments of women, feathered and ribboned head-dresses, garters, frills, flowers, ruffles, etc., and deport themselves as women. Standing or seated on a pedestal, but accessible to all the rest, is the naked queen (a male), whose phallic member, decorated with a ribbon, is subject to the gaze and osculations in turn of all the members of this lecherous gang of sexual perverts and phallic fornicators.

CHARLES H. HUGHES, 1893
An Organization of Colored Erotopaths

In the female invert mentally and psychically we have a man with all the powerful desires of a man; hence, while anatomically and socially we have a woman, the physical development will be such as to make the individual a good risk, and also, being classed as a female, however much her masculine tendencies may be objectionable, she is usually free from personal assaults, and the alcohol that she drinks seems to have a better physiological absorbing surface.

WILLIAM LEE HOWARD, 1906

If I were to have a play put on in which women had roles, I would demand that these roles be performed by adolescent boys, and I would bring this to the attention of the spectators by means of a placard which would remain nailed to the right or left of the sets during the entire performance.

JEAN GENET (1910-86)

Some ... men impersonate women on the cheap vaudeville stage, in connection with disorderly saloons. Their disguise is so perfect, they are enabled to sit at tables with men between the acts, and solicit for drinks the same as prostitutes.

Chicago Vice Commission, 1911

I wish that the gays would get away from riding around in Cadillac convertibles, especially the fat ones that look like travesties of Mae West, and just camping it up on the streets in public view.

TENNESSEE WILLIAMS (1912-83)

I have thought for some time, I was possessed of a female spirit, or a female soul inhabited my body. If I am a man, why is it that some men wish to have sexual relations with me? Is it a chemical affinity or a mental attraction, or something else attracts them?

PROFESSOR M, 1914
pioneer American transvestite/educator

Wilde's mother had for nine long months, before he was born, prayed continually for a girl. Her imagination dwelt upon this during nearly all her pregnancy. That her prayer was partially granted in that perplexing mixture of artist, man, woman, and egotist the world knows as Oscar Wilde was perhaps one of Nature's satires in order to show what we do when we force, through our limited laws and barbaric persecutions, these peculiar people into becoming menaces to the State through lack of capacity either to understand them or to educate them.

EDITH ELLIS, 1915

Girls will be boys, you know.

POSTCARD, c. 1925
depicting two flappers lighting their cigarettes
together

There's two things got me puzzled, there's two things I
don't understand;
That's a mannish-acting woman, and a skipping, twistin'
woman-acting man.
BESSIE SMITH, 1927

For God's sake! What's that?
HAROLD ROSS, 1945
on seeing Truman Capote for the first time in the
office of the *New Yorker*

'I am a boy.'
JOSE SARRIA, 1953
urging drag queens to pin a note on their dresses with
this message to foil police and prosecutors in their
efforts to arrest drag queens for posing as members of
the opposite sex

An individual's gender role and orientation as boy or girl,
man or woman, does not have an innate, performed
instinctive basis as some theorists have maintained. Instead
the evidence supports the view that psychologic sex is
undifferentiated at birth – a sexual neutrality one might say
– and that the individual becomes psychologically
differentiated as masculine or feminine in the course of the
many experiences of growing up.
JOHN L. HAMPSON, 1955

Even in the sexual sphere, the Lesbian remains essentially
feminine, with the natural desires and reactions of a
woman.
DR EDWARD DENGROVE, 1957

Drag is dirty work, but someone has to do it!
CHARLES PIERCE, 1960s

The little boy who not only occasionally dresses up in his mother's scarves and jewelry and shoes but would wear girls' clothes exclusively if permitted to do so; who consistently avoids boys' rough-and-tumble sports, preferring to organize a group of little girls into a game in which he invariably assigns himself the role of 'mother'; who is, indeed, a startling mimic of his own mother's speech patterns and mannerisms and displays a marked interest in all her domestic activities; who always sits down to urinate, and frequently expresses the wish that his penis will drop off or somehow disappear; and who repeatedly insists that he is a girl and stages uncontrollable temper tantrums when he is contradicted – this child is certainly flashing the strongest of warning signals.
HARRIET SLAVITZ, 1964

Once I was taken to a nightclub and I said, 'I have never seen so many beautiful women in my life.' My escort said, 'Those aren't women, they're men.' I was puzzled for days after.
HEDY LAMARR, 1966

We didn't go for a gay concept when we put the show together. We went for a totally male, masculine celebration – that men can get there and feel their tits and do bumps and grinds and still remain men. Narcissism is a good thing. Everyone does it, I don't care what they say. Everyone gets off on mirror-tripping.
DAVID 'SCAR' HODO, 1970s
band member of the Village People

Transsexual dressing is a gay contribution to the realization that we're not a hundred percent masculine or feminine, but a mixture of hormones.

ALLEN GINSBERG, 1970s

I decided that if I was going to be labeled a queen, I would be the biggest, best queen there was.

JOSE SARRIA, 1970s

Said Jane to her mother, 'I fear
My husband's turned into a queer.
On Sundays and Mondays
He irons all my undies,
And he secretly wears my brassiere.'

LIMERICK, 1970s

It's a bitch to be butch.

T-SHIRT SLOGAN, 1970s

YENTL'S FATHER: Yentl – you have the soul of a man.
YENTL: So, why was I born a woman?
FATHER: Even heaven makes mistakes.

ISAAC BASHEVIS SINGER, 1970s
Yentl the Yeshiva Boy

I'm the real Yentl, except I would have known what to do with Amy Irving.

LYNN LAVNER, 1988

Women who are camp have donated, whether they know it or not, courage and bits of wisdom to the homosexual effeminate who often imitates them.

BRUCE RODGERS, 1972

GERALDO RIVERA: Please answer me. What *are* you? Are you a woman trapped in a man's body? Are you a heterosexual? Are you a homosexual? A transvestite? A transsexual? *What* is the answer to the question?

HOLLY WOODLAWN: But, darling, what difference does it *make* as long as you look fabulous?

HOLLY WOODLAWN, 1976
ABC-TV talk show

Neither male nor female sexuality is limited by 'genital geography', and it has been one of the greatest public relations victories of all time to convince us it was. The very naturalness of lesbianism (and homosexuality) is exactly the cause of the strong social and legal rules against it. The basis of our social system on gender difference, biological reproductive function, is barbaric and should be replaced by a system based on affirmation of the individual and support for all life on the planet.

SEXOLOGIST, 1976

'Drag', as we dub it these days, is commonly thought of as a homosexual pursuit, though this is hardly the case, in our culture or any other. Ancient cultures abound in examples of transvestism, from Aztec shamans to Persian catamites. American Indian cultures often had berdashes, or crossdressers. Today, we have high school jocks getting up in drag for the senior frolics, and major comedy stars appear [in] crinolines with domestic regularity. Drag, whether it be for television comedy or ritual emasculation, occurs in too many areas of human society to be considered merely a homosexual pastime.

DENNIS SANDERS, 1977

I'm the number-one queen in town now.
> HARVEY MILK (1930-78)
> after his election to Mayor Moscone regarding his
> wish to be consulted in all offical gay issues

The man who wants to show what sex he is shouldn't wear clothes.
> JOHN TAYLOR, 1966
> fashion journalist

Girls got balls. They're just a little higher up, that's all.
> JOAN JETT, 1979

People already think I'm that way – homo – because of my voice, and I'm not.
> MICHAEL JACKSON, 1979
> explaining his rejection of the role of a gay dancer in
> the film *A Chorus Line*

If little girls want to grow up and marry Michael, now they know they've got a chance.
> PRESS AGENT TO MICHAEL JACKSON
> at a press conference called to halt rumours that
> Michael was gay and took hormones, 1980s

He didn't look feminine. Didn't look like a pretty woman. He looked like a woman who had been hit with a board and didn't get well.
> LITTLE RICHARD, 1980s
> commenting on a friend in drag

There are easier things in this life than being a drag queen.
But, I ain't got no choice. Try as I may, I just can't walk in
flats.

HARVEY FIERSTEIN, 1981
Arnold, in *Torch Song Trilogy*

Hermaphrodite is the term used for the anomaly of the two
sex organs in one creature. Androgyne is the more symbolic
word. It refers to the original unity of everything, the
concept of a divine creature being both masculine and
feminine and hence difference from both of these.

JAMES BROUGHTON, 1982

Camp is a homosexual sensibility with a soupçon of
weariness.

NED ROREM, 1982

A prenatal hormonal mixup can certainly produce a
homosexual child. They often have delicate features,
smooth and nearly hairless faces, and high-pitched voices.
They walk like females and have feminine mannerisms.
They love to be around women, learn to make up their
faces while very young, and can do wonders with their own
hair and the hair of others. They would prefer to be with
girls rather than with boys.

ANN LANDERS, 1983

Thank you, America. You've got good taste, style, and you
know a good drag queen when you see one.

BOY GEORGE, 1984

Boy George is all England needs – another queen who can't
dress.

JOAN RIVERS, 1980s

'HOLLYWOOD SQUARES' HOST: Why do motorcyclists
wear leather?
PAUL LYNDE: Because chiffon wrinkles too easily, that's
why.
PAUL LYNDE (1926-82)

Of course men will wear skirts. It is coming. Among more
of the young generation the codification of what is
masculinity has changed a lot. You don't wear your
masculinity. You are masculine or you are not – it is not the
clothes that make you masculine or feminine.
JEAN-PAUL GAULTIER, 1984

Women are all female impersonators to some degree.
SUSAN BROWNMILLER, 1984

I'd like any role that would stretch me, where I was
credible. But I'm not about to drag myself up in leather or
in chiffon.
ROCK HUDSON (1925-85)

I realize that I've done a lot of female impersonation. In
many ways, what I did was to experiment and use it for
different theatrical purposes by putting a tremendous
emphasis upon the context in which it is used. Now a man
or a woman might be better at evoking a specific type of
personality, or it might make a specific point in the play,
since gender reversal creates a Chinese box effect – we
don't know what's real or unreal.
CHARLES LUDLAM, 1985

[Pee-wee Herman] argues against compulsory polarization of the sexes by summoning up a child's androgyny. Being just a kid allows Pee-wee and his pals to play with gender codes unnoticed, and therefore all the more subversively.
    BARRY WALTERS, 1985

Did Mae West invent drag queens, or did drag queens invent Mae West?
    MICHAEL BRONSKI, 1985

Fag hag is surely a cruel term for women who exist on a spectrum that consists of many degrees of closeness to male homosexuals – and denotes strictly the tough, party-hearty women who mystify by their insistent following of male homosexual society. We all know some. We have seen in their lives every conceivable denouement to the situation, besides.
    ANDREW HOLLERAN, 1986

Lesbians are first and foremost women.
    LAURA S. BROWN, 1986

Life is a drag, you know – then you become one!
    CHARLES PIERCE, 1987
    female impersonator

It's much easier for men to do drag. For a woman to be in male drag and claim that power, it's not funny. For boys to be girls is hysterical.
    PEGGY SHAW, 1988

I didn't want to mimic a woman, but to use that as a vehicle – actually, it was a way of getting out a lot of rage.

JOHN KELLY, 1988
dancer/impersonator

Lee [Liberace] was the daddy of rhinestones and sequins – all the stuff the kids in rock are using today. He knew people called him a flaming faggot, but he didn't care. He knew that the most boring thing in the world was a piano player. He created a great game of suspense among people, making them think, *What's he going to wear this time?*

RAY ARNETT, 1988
Liberace's friend and co-worker

Every man should own at least one dress, and so should lesbians.

REVD JANE ADAMS SPAHR, 1988

Health

Nature has poisoned the pleasures of love and sources of life over three-quarters of the world by a terrible disease, to which man alone is subject, and which infects only his organs of procreation.

It is not the same plague as with other diseases, which are the natural consequences of excess. It was not introduced by debauchery. The Phrynes and Laises, the Floras and Messalinas were never attacked by it. It originated in the islands where men lived together in innocence, and thence spread throughout the Old World.

VOLTAIRE, (1694-1778)

The sick do not ask if the hand that smooths their pillow is pure, nor the dying care if the lips that touch their brow have known the kiss of sin.

OSCAR WILDE (1854-1900)
A Woman of No Importance

Who would not rather have his son contract a bad heart or hernia than to see him a sexual pervert?

IRVING C. ROSSE, 1892

If a killing type of virus strain should suddenly arise by mutation ... it could, because of the rapid transportation in which we indulge nowadays, be carried to the far corners of the earth and cause the deaths of millions of people.

W.M. STANLEY (1904-71)

A pestilence isn't a thing made to man's measure; therefore we tell ourselves that pestilence is a mere bogey of the mind, a bad dream that will pass away. But it doesn't always pass away, and from one bad dream to another, it is men who pass away.

ALBERT CAMUS (1913-60)
The Plague

Go and give it to the dogs.

ROCK HUDSON (1925-85)
to his publicist regarding the disclosure to reporters that 'Mr Rock Hudson Has Acquired Immune Deficiency Syndrome'

His [Rock Hudson's] illness and death have moved the fight against AIDS ahead more in three months than anything in the past three years.

BRUCE DECKER, 1980s
chairman, California AIDS Advisory Board

Cover me, I'm going in.

T-SHIRT SLOGAN, 1980s
caption beneath a picture of a penis

One effect of gay liberation is that sex has been institutionalized and franchised. Twenty years ago, there may have been a thousand men on any one night having sex in New York baths or parks. Now there are ten or twenty thousand – at the baths, the back-room bars, bookstores, porno theaters, the Rambles, and a wide range of other places as well. The plethora of opportunities poses a public health problem that's growing with every new bath in town.

DAN WILLIAM, 1980

Already, a Manhattan gay newspaper, *New York Native*, had published a story about the rumors of a new killer pneumonia striking gay men, but the ... liaison with the local health department had pooh-poohed the gossip, telling the paper that the rumors were 'unfounded'.

RANDY SHILTS, 1981

I am encouraging the use of condoms – eroticizing the use of rubbers. When I am at a place like the Mineshaft, I make a big display of the use of a rubber – putting it on myself and my partner. I know it is not the 'real thing' – it is a taste of rubber – but the overriding fear of disease affects my enjoyment of sex, and thus it is a reasonable alternative.

RICHARD LOCKE, 1984
former porn star/gay activist

AIDS is evidence that Thanatos is not only a killing god, he is a mocking god: not only must we die, but we must die slowly, painfully, and fearfully from this new leprosy. And we are driven to wonder if man is, after all, a useless passion who dies by mere chance.

TIMOTHY MURPHY, 1985

If AIDS has taught us anything, it is that we are the most tenacious, inspired, creative, caring, committed survivors on the face of this earth.

RODGER MCFARLANE, 1985
former exective director, Gay Men's Health Crisis

Remember: there's no such thing as a homosexual disease. When heterosexuals start having sex again, they'll get it too.

HARVEY FIERSTEIN, 1985

At a time when some would have us go back into the closet, and others would have us focus all our energies on the crises surrounding AIDS, many of us are finding a way to continue living our lives with self-respect, dignity and verve.

ERIC E. ROFES, 1985

If gay men recognize AIDS as a sexually transmissible disease to be avoided at all costs, what good are the guidelines that include a whole set of 'maybe's'?

MICHAEL HELQUIST, 1985

No longer does one hanker for the mere image of health; one is now utterly determined to achieve and keep it. Because of the unpredictable nature of AIDS as well as the undeniable stress of this end of the century, the object now is a deep serenity bred by perfect balance, the peace of mind that manifests itself in a relaxed, fluid body and a rich, hearty soul.

PAUL REED, 1985

Along with the rest of the nation, gay men's interest in good health and general overall self-improvement is a recent phenomenon. But this new interest appears to be serious – bodybuilding is here to stay. Witness the large number of general purpose gyms as well as numerous 'gay' gyms which continue to thrive and expand.

ROY F. WOOD, 1985

We're not talking about a nightmare that is going to happen. It already is a nightmare.

MICHAEL LANGE, 1985
AIDS specialist

I am tired of compiling lists of the dead. They are actors and writers and designers and dancers and editors and retailers and decorators... The dead are homosexuals who have contracted and will perish from AIDS. Almost everyone who knew them knows this, but there is a gentle, loving conspiracy of silence to deny reality ... Men are dying and we in the press cough politely and draw the curtains of discretion across the truth. Don't hurt anyone. Protect a name, a family, a reputation. A memory. So we write white lies about the cause of death ... Can lies *be* a cause of death?

JAMES BRADY, 1985

We hope for a time when scientific breakthroughs and gay creativity will furnish new ways to be freely and safely sexual with other men – and gay monogamy will be a freely chosen option and not an act of self-preservation.

PHIL NASH, 1986

Despite what we know about AIDS, you just think people will never die.

ANTHONY PERKINS, 1986

There is nothing wrong with being a safe-sex slut.

PAT CALIFIA, 1987

People aren't just *dying* with AIDS, people are *living* with AIDS.

DAVID BELL, 1987

She was in Ward 5B, the first woman on the AIDS Ward, staring at the stark landscape outside her window and wondering how a tryst with a bisexual man several years before had brought her here.

RANDY SHILTS, 1987

The city recently released a long-term AIDS plan, prepared by the Interagency Task Force on AIDS, made up of seven city agencies. It is a sensible but sobering document reinforcing the perception that AIDS is the principal public health crisis of this generation.

EDWARD I. KOCH
Major of New York, 1988

I would particularly caution gays to avoid joining studies that are conducted by direct agencies of the US government (such as veterans hospitals), as opposed to studies conducted in universities with review committees in place.

The price of survival is eternal vigilance.

ROBERT G. BODELL, 1988

In the name of humanity, I pledge to resist medical Nazism.
>CHARLES L. ORTLEB
>publisher of *New York Native*, 1988 from 'The People's Hippocratic Oath'

AIDS is not a police issue, it's a health issue.
>RICHARD RUDELL, 1988

Silence = Death
>AIDS rights slogan, 1988

For this much love, care, and compassion to come out of this community because of AIDS proves that we truly are a people of incredible love. We're going to be a better community because of this.
>LEONARD MATLOVICH, 1988

Homophobia has for centuries killed us. All those projected fears and anxieties are turning back on heterosexuals and will kill them. They will die of their own prejudice because they will not pay attention to the warnings about AIDS we have given them.
>SIMON WATNEY, 1988

I believe San Francisco will be remembered not for its losses but for its contributions to the AIDS crisis. We are a model for AIDS care and caring. People from all over the world come here to find out what we've learned and how we're coping.
>ART AGNOS, 1988
>Mayor of San Francisco

Condoms, even when used conventionally (in vaginal intercourse), have a failure rate of about 10 percent. When used for anal intercourse, they can break as often as 50 percent of the time.

If both propositions are true, having anal intercourse with a condom is rather like Russian roulette, isn't it?

JOHN LAURITSEN, 1988

Doctor People Not Numbers.

DEMONSTRATION PLACARD SLOGAN
for AIDS Coalition to Unleash Power (ACT UP),
1988

I would hate it if a kid of mine got a blood transfusion, if my grandson had AIDS, and the community discriminated against that ... innocent child, particularly when the [commission's] report concludes ... that AIDS ... cannot ... be transmitted by ways that some had feared ... This is a national health problem. We're talking about children, innocent victims.

PRESIDENT GEORGE BUSH, 1988

The war against AIDS [is] the greatest public health emergency of our lifetimes.

MICHAEL DUKAKIS, 1988

Put on that love glove, baby
Don't be shy.

CHARLIE MURPHY, 1988

Like the Vietnam Memorial, with its endless etchings in dark marble, the Quilt is awesome in its very scope. It displays the magnitude of the epidemic. Most important, it memorializes those who are gone and records their names as personalities, not as statistics.

JOHN PRESTON, 1988

The biggest crime involved with AIDS has been the failure to get drugs tested quickly.

MARTIN DELANEY, 1988
cofounder of Project Inform, an AIDS information organization

I think in fifty years, when this catastrophe is all over, we will look back on this as our Holocaust, and we should feel the same anger that the survivors of the Holocaust still feel, and we should demand the same shame that the world should feel about the Holocaust.

PAUL MONETTE, 1988

AIDS is this generation's Vietnam.

RICHARD GOLDSTEIN, 1988

People who get AIDS from homosexual activities or illegal drug activities certainly don't deserve – certainly won't get – my sympathy.

EMORY FOLMAR, 1988

Homophobia

It is better to be hated for what one is than to be loved for what one isn't.

ANDRÉ GIDE (1869-1951)

I can remember that not so long ago George M. Cohan, and other super he-men, regarded the wristwatch as an emblem of pansiness.

PERCY HAMMOND (1873-1936)

Of the abnormal sexual manifestations that one encounters, none, perhaps, is so enigmatical and to the average person so abhorrent as homosexuality. I have discussed this subject with many broadminded, intelligent professional men and laymen and have been surprised to hear how utterly disgusted they become at the very mention of the name and how little they understand the whole problem ... *Tout comprendre c'est tout pardonner* [To understand everything is to forgive everything] ... I have met and studied a large number of homosexuals and have been convinced that a great injustice is done to a large class of human beings, most of whom are far from being the degenerates they are commonly believed to be.

A.A. BRILL (1874-1948)

What the public really loathes in homosexuality is not the thing itself but having to think about it.

E.M. FORSTER (1879-1970)

One thing is true. Our loves bear as fair and noble flowers, incite to as praiseworthy efforts as does the love of any man for the woman of his affections. There are the same sacrifices, the same pain, the same joy, sorrow, happiness, as with men of ordinary natures ...

May the time soon come when science shall educate the people so that they shall rightly judge our unfortunate class, but before that time can come there will be many victims.

LETTER OF ANONYMOUS MERCHANT WHO EMIGRATED TO AMERICA FOLLOWING HIS ARREST FOR HOMOSEXUALITY, 1882

Defective genital organs.

FIORELLO LA GUARDIA (1882-1947)
to the press regarding the cause of lesbianism

There are millions of women, sedate in nature, who never heard of a lesbian, much less believing that such people exist. And many men, too.

VARIETY
from a review of the play *The Captive*, October 8, 1926

[It's] worse than throwing acid in a young person's eyes.

JUDICIAL STATEMENT

regarding *The Well of Loneliness*, by Radclyffe Hall, 1928

STUDIO ADVISER: You can't film that [*The Well of Loneliness*]. It's about lesbians.
GOLDWYN: All right. Where they got lesbians, we'll use Austrians.
SAMUEL GOLDWYN (1882-1974)

The Greeks, of course, had no sexual morals whatever, and not many of any other kind, and Sappho, in these respects, was simply the product of her environment ... The world as she knew it did not look on homosexualism as reprehensible.
FLORENCE FINCH KELLY, 1932

Whatever the public blames you for, cultivate it: it is yourself.
JEAN COCTEAU (1889-1963)

I'm not willing just to be tolerated. That wounds my love of love and of liberty.
JEAN COCTEAU (1889-1963)

A homosexual is a female soul in a male body. 'You're hitting a woman,' I says.
MAE WEST (1892-1980)
her plea to New York City police to curb beatings of homosexuals

Heterosexual society dominates [the homosexual] and leads him more or less cunningly to execution.
JEAN-PAUL SARTRE (1905-80)

Everyone knows about everybody in Hollywood – who sleeps with whom, who doesn't sleep, who does it standing on his head or in the dentist's chair. And some of those guys just don't like fairies.

ROCK HUDSON (1925-85)

Movies were anti-gay. Movies *are* anti-gay. And movies will continue to be anti-gay.

ROCK HUDSON (1925-85)

People do not take the relations between men and boys seriously ... They do not believe there can be tears between men. They think we are only playing at a game and that we do it to shock them.

JAMES BALDWIN (1924-87)

The myth and misconception with which homosexuality has so long been clothed must be cleared away, not to condone it but to cope with it.

LIFE MAGAZINE, 1964

The love that dare not speak its name has become the neurosis that does not know when to shut up.

TIME MAGAZINE, 1964
on reviewing 'still another fictional treatment of homosexuality'

The most frequently described grievance is the prejudice most homosexuals find in heterosexuals. Antihomosexual feeling among the masses of Americans cannot be our ultimate problem; in fact straight people too are harmed by rigid, stereotyped ideas about sex and sex-roles.

CHICAGO GAY LIBERATION FOR THE REVOLUTIONARY
PEOPLE'S CONSTITUTIONAL CONVENTION
working paper, 1970

One vagina plus another vagina equals zero.

DAVID REUBEN, 1972

Homosexuality isn't funny. Sometimes anything can be a source of humor, but the lives of twenty million Americans are not a joke.

GAY ACTIVISTS ALLIANCE AND NATIONAL GAY TASK
FORCE, 1973

Are you disconcerted by an intelligent lesbian?

MAX FRISCH, 1974

Gayness is even scarier to people than femaleness or blackness.

JOHN LOMBARDI, 1975

Any woman who feels actual horror or revulsion at the thought of kissing or embracing or having physical relations with another woman should re-examine her feelings and attitudes not only about other women, but also about *herself.*

SHERE HITE, 1976

We will not contribute by bigotry or by silence to the ongoing persecution of our Gay daughters and sons.

PARENTS OF GAY MEN AND LESBIAN WOMEN, 1977

The Myth of the Homosexual says that there exists a person defined by sexual attraction toward people of the same biological gender. This myth serves an essential function in the preservation of culture: It denies the reality, the legitimacy, of the culture-destroying vision of the so-called homosexual, and it does this by restricting that person's essence and meaningfulness to distinct sexual acts performed with other persons of the same sex. The purpose of this myth has been, and is, to rob gay people of the power inherent in them to destroy the established order and replace it according to their vision.

MITCH WALKER, 1980s

Are you my alternative?

FLORYNCE KENNEDY, 1980s
when asked by a male heckler, 'Are you a lesbian?'

If I had to kiss a costar – because the disease is crossing over into the straight world – I'd want assurances he doesn't have AIDS. You have to protect yourself.

JOAN RIVERS, 1984

Homophobia, for all the changes in society and human discourse since the Middle Ages, remains fervent.

ANDREW HOLLERAN, 1988

Few words are as guaranteed to set of an explosion of fear in her belly as the word *bulldike* when it is used on a woman like a whip.

JUDITH GRAHN, 1984

The rhetoric of right-wing zealots is sweeping across the country, providing pious justification for violence against gays. That violence is increasing daily – from tauntings and beatings to arson and even murder.

NATIONAL GAY TASK FORCE
advertisement, 1985

Children learn antipathy for homosexuals at home: It's as right as love. If a boy finds out he isn't drawn to girls but rather falls in love with other boys, he's learned to hate himself. He knows he is a fag. Other disrespected groups of people – Blacks, Jews, women – though they suffer stigma and injustice, learn at least a feeble sense of self-worth and belonging from their families. At worst they have a meager social place. Fags have none.

DARRELL YATES RIST, 1985

As you've probably noticed from reports in the gay press, attacks against gay people have been on the increase all over America. But did you also know that in 1981 the Radical Right spent over 2.5 million dollars a month to stir up hate primarily against lesbians and gay men through propaganda and legislation?

THE FUND FOR HUMAN DIGNITY
advertisement, 1985

It's no wonder ... homosexuals are so despised. They offer no comforting promise to women. They pledge no unified purpose with heterosexual men.

DARRELL YATES RIST, 1985

Someday we may feel free to live anywhere we choose. In the meantime, thank God for ghettos.

GREG JACKSON, 1986

Society uses all gay people who participate in gay culture for special purposes. We are closely watched to see what constitutes the limit of a thing – too far out, too much, too low, too bad, too outrageous, too soft, too dangerous, too rough, too cultured, too aggressive, too sexual. One of the strongest measures heterosexual culture has is how close each of its members comes to being 'like a faggot' or 'like a dyke'. We are essential to them knowing who they are.

JUDITH GRAHN, 1987

Suppose every able-bodied man between eighteen and eighty, after a period of training, was enrolled in a volunteer street patrol. He could give eight hours of his time once every two weeks to volunteer work. Such patrols could wipe crime off the streets of America, since they would outnumber the muggers, rapists and queer-bashers twenty to one.

WILLIAM S. BURROUGHS, 1987

The theme song of *The Flintstones*, which has long ended with the line 'We'll have a gay old time!' tra-la-la, has suddenly been changed. The famous last line now says: 'We'll have a great old time!'

MELBOURNE *HERALD*, 1987

We can't distort and corrupt gay culture to adapt to bigotry.

SARAH SCHULMAN, 1988

Women aren't nearly as hysterical about lesbians as men are about gays. That's because women aren't nearly as hysterical about proving they're 100 percent heterosexual. Some confused men, however, remain forever traumatized by that fateful day in ninth grade when Coach came by and patted them on the behind, and, alas, they kinda liked it.

MARGERY EAGAN, 1988

It's tremendously empowering when you're gay to realize that you've been doing it right, and it's the bigots who are stumbling about in a fog.

HOWARD CRUSE, 1988

The fellow who dies of sodomy is no more special than the fellow who dies of two packs of cigarettes a day. Let us apportion our tears, and our tax dollars, with some sense of proportion.

JAMES J. KILPATRICK, 1988

We say, 'Praise God for AIDS.'

JOHN BAUMGARDNER, 1988

'Queer' is frequently loaded with hatefulness by the person who utters it. There's nothing to be gained by gays sugarcoating hatred. 'Queer' should be a reminder of society's disdain for gays. There are better names to call ourselves.

DAVE WALTER, 1988

At family dinners, when talk turns to 'fags', I often wonder what would happen if – instead of staring silently into my mashed potatoes – I were to make a plea for gay rights, finally solving the mystery of my 'celibacy'.

JAMES MERRETT, 1988

More black gay men, with the education and the skills, should devote their time and energy toward reclaiming inner-city neighborhoods, thereby helping to eliminate some of the black homophobia and setting an example for the community. That is far more important than trying to force white people to love and/or accept us.

CHARLES MICHAEL SMITH, 1988

The greater the horror of homosexuals, the easier it is to make young men sweat and fight by calling them 'sissy' or 'fag'. The cult of homophobia helps insure that poor, uneducated, young males provide Muscle for work and for war. It also keeps them out of art, culture, college, and white-collar jobs – by their own 'choice'.

JAY LEMKE, 1988

I have decorated this banner to honor my brother.
Our parents did not want his name used publicly.
The omission of his name represents
the fear of oppression that AIDS victims and their
     families feel.

ANONYMOUS, 1988
Quilt panel submitted to NAMES Project honouring
anonymous person who died of AIDS

Love and Marriage

'If you forget me, think
of our gifts to Aphrodite
and all the loveliness that we shared.'
SAPPHO (612? BC-580? BC)

Human nature was originally one and we were a whole, and
the desire and pursuit of the whole is called love.
PLATO (427? BC-347? BC)

Far from the tender Tribe of Boys remove,
For they've a thousand ways to kindle Love.
TIBULLUS (between 60 and 48 BC-19 BC)

A double brightness burned me: rays
There were which travelled in the gaze
Of that boy's eyes, the beams of Love;
And others from the Sun above.
MELEAGER (1st century BC)

True love has nothing to do with women's quarters, nor will I agree that you have ever felt *love* for women or girls, any more than flies feel love for milk.

    PLUTARCH (46?-120)

> 'Tomorrow with the dawn I must attend
> In yonder vale.' 'What for?' 'Why ask? A friend
> Takes him a husband there and bids a few
> Be present.' Wait awhile and we shall view
> Such contracts formed without shame or fear
> And entered on the records of the year.
>
>   JUVENAL (60?-140?)

If a man urge me to tell wherefore I loved him, I feel it cannot be expressed, but by answering: Because it was he, because it was my self.

    MICHEL DE MONTAIGNE (1533-92)

> A woman's face with nature's own hand painted,
> Hast thou the master mistress of my passion,
> A woman's gentle heart but not acquainted
> With shifting change as is false women's fashion,
> An eye more bright than theirs, less false in rolling:
> Gilding the object whereupon it gazeth,
> A man in hue all hues in his controlling,
> Which steals men's eyes and women's souls amazeth.
> And for a woman wert thou first created,
> Till nature as she wrought thee fell a-doting,
> And by addition me of thee defeated,
> By adding one thing to my purpose nothing.
>   But since she pricked thee out for women's pleasure,
>   Mine be thy love and thy love's use their treasure.
> WILLIAM SHAKESPEARE (1564-1616)

I am neither a god nor an angel, but a man like any other, and confess to loving those dear to me more than other men ... Christ had his John, and I have my Steenie.
    KING JAMES I (1566-1625)

And what is she (quoth he) whom thou do'st love?
    Looke in this glasse (quoth I) there shalt thou see
    The perfect forme of my faelicitie.
When, thinking that it would strange Magique prove,
    He open'd it: and taking of the cover,
    He straight perceav'd himselfe to be my Lover.
    RICHARD BARNFIELD (1574-1627)

I thee, both as man and woman, prize;
For a perfect love implies
Love in all capacities.
    ABRAHAM COWLEY (1618-67)

Change everything except your loves.
    VOLTAIRE (1694-1778)

I would not part from her side, but ate and slept, walked and mused and read, with my arm locked in hers, and with her breath fanning my cheek ... O precious inebriation of the heart! O pre-eminent love!
    CHARLES BROCKDEN BROWN (1771-1810)
    the female narrator, in *Ormond*

Oh! What a wonderful mixture of emotions transports me! I feel nature! I feel friendship! How strongly my entire soul rejoices in both! Truly Emilia, I believe friendship is stronger than love!

    ELISABETH MARIA POST (1775-1812)
    Eufrosyne to Emilia, from *Her Land*, or *The Countryside*

Listen, lady,
    For very womanhood, We are of one age,
One country, and one sex; defenceless women!
    ... Oh, shall we not be true
To one another? Save me! Save me! Once
Thou lovedst thine own poor handmaid!

    MARY RUSSELL MITFORD (1787-1855)
    Inez to Constance, in *Inez de Castro*

The power of love consists mainly in the privilege that Potentate possesses of coining, circulating, and making current those falsehoods between man and women, that would not pass for one moment, either between woman and woman, or man and man.

    CHARLES CALEB COLTON (1780?-1832)

My love and ambition for you often seems to be more like that of a mother for a son, or a father for a daughter (the two fondest of natural emotions) than the common bonds of even a close friendship between two women of different ages and similar pursuits ... It is a strange feeling, but one of indescribable pleasure.

    MARY RUSSELL MITFORD (1787-1855)
    letter to Elizabeth Barrett

I could love anything on earth that appeared to wish it.
LORD BYRON (1788-1824)

There are two hearts whose movements thrill
    In unison so closely sweet,
That pulse to pulse responsive still,
    They both must heave, or cease to beat.

There are two souls whose equal flow
    In gentle stream so calmly run,
That when they part – they part? – ah no!
    They cannot part – those souls are one.
LORD BYRON (1788-1824)

Ours too the glance none saw beside;
    The smile one else might understand;
The whisper'd thought of hearts allied,
    The pressure of the thrilling hand;
The kiss so guiltless and refin'd
    That Love each warmer wish forbore;
Those eyes proclaim'd so pure a mind,
    Ev'n passion blush'd to plead for more.
LORD BYRON (1788-1824)

The nature of love and friendship is very little understood, and the distinction between them ill-established. This latter feeling – at least, a profound and sentimental attachment to one of the same sex – often precedes the former. It is not right to say, merely, that friendship is exempt from the smallest alloy of sensuality.
PERCY BYSSHE SHELLEY (1792-1822)

Sweet boy, gentle boy,
Don't be ashamed, you are mine forever:
The same rebellious fire is in both of us,
We are living one life.

I am not afraid of mockery:
Between us, the two have become one,
We are precisely like a double nut
Under a single shell.
ALEXANDER PUSHKIN (1799-1837)

A glimpse through an interstice caught,
Of a crowd of workmen and drivers in a bar-room around
    the stove late of a winter night, and I unremark'd
    seated in a corner,
Of a youth who loves me and whom I love, silently
    approaching and seating himself near, that he may
    hold me by the hand,
A long while amid the noises of coming and going, of
    drinking and oath and smutty jest,
There we two, content, happy in being together,
    speaking little, perhaps not a word.
WALT WHITMAN (1819-92)

The divine magnet is on you, and my magnet responds.
Which is the biggest? A foolish question – they are *One*.
HERMAN MELVILLE (1819-91)
    letter to Nathanial Hawthorne

Her breast is fit for pearls,
But I was not a 'Diver' –
Her brow is fit for thrones
But I have not a crest.
Her heart is fit for *home* –
I – a Sparrow – build there
Sweet of twigs and twine
My perennial nest.
>   EMILY DICKINSON (1830-86)

Full well I knew, though decency forbad
The same caresses to a rustic lad;
Love, love it was, that made my eyes delight
To have his person ever in my sight.
>   ENGLISH POET, 1833
>   from *Don Leon*, a purported autobiographical poem of
>   Byron's life

Oh! 'tis hard to trace
The line where love usurps tame friendship's place.
Friendship's the chrysalis, which seems to die,
But throws its coils to give love wing to fly.
>   ENGLISH POET, 1833
>   from *Don Leon*, a purported autobiographical poem of
>   Byron's life

Other attachments followed, so much less restful than
friendships, that I cannot fairly call them by that consoling
name. Their objects were good women all, thank God! and
the only trouble was not that we loved unwisely, but too
well.
>   FRANCES E. WILLARD (1839-98)

The loves of women for each other grow more numerous each day, and I have pondered much why these things were. That so little should be said about them surprises me, for they are everywhere ... There is no village that has not its examples of 'two hearts in counsel', both of which are feminine. Oftentimes these joint proprietors have been unfortunately married, and so have failed to 'better their condition' until, thus clasping hands, they have taken each other 'for better or for worse'.

FRANCES E. WILLARD (1839-98)

I love him like I love a young woman.

EDVARD GRIEG (1843-1907)
comment in his journal about Percy Granger,
American composer

It is often said how necessary for the ordinary marriage is some public recognition of the relation, and some accepted standard of conduct in it. May not, to a lesser degree, something of the same kind be true of the homogenic attachment? It has had its place as a recognized and guarded institution in the elder and more primitive societies; and it seems quite probable that a similar place will be accorded to it in the societies of the future.

EDWARD CARPENTER (1844-1929)

The only difference between a caprice and a life-long passion is that the caprice lasts a little longer.

OSCAR WILDE (1854-1900)

The sight of a beautiful youth awakens astonishment in the lover, and opens the door to his heart to the delight which contemplation of this loveliness affords. Love takes possession of him so completely that all his thought and feeling goes out in it. If he finds himself in the presence of the beloved, he rests absorbed in gazing on him. Absent, he thinks of nought but him.

ALBANIAN MOUNTAIN TRIBESMAN, 1853

For my part you are always in me. Are we no longer to live happily together? Only follow the feelings of your heart.

ARTHUR RIMBAUD (1854-91)

To love oneself is the beginning of a life-long romance.

OSCAR WILDE (1854-1900)
Phrases and Philosophies for the Use of the Young

EDWARD CARSON, prosecutor at Wilde's trial: Have you ever adored a young man madly?
OSCAR WILDE: No, not madly: I prefer love – that is a higher form.

OSCAR WILDE (1854-1900)

You never know a man until you know how he loves.

SIGMUND FREUD (1856-1939)

He would not stay for me; and who can wonder?
He would not stay for me to stand and gaze.
I shook his hand and tore my heart in sunder
And went with half my life about my ways.

A.E. HOUSMAN (1859-1936)

Thus twice hath friendship barred the way
to what I hoped for most of all;
But what is love, if it obey
not friendship's call?

EDWARD PERRY WARREN (1860-1936)

Years and years I have fear'd the shame
   And the cruel speech of the world.
But over our heads in the darkness now
   Is the banner of love unfurl'd,
(Lean closer, cling to me, kiss my lips,
   Our love can despise the world.)
   GABRIEL GILLET (1863-?)

Suspicious of my simplest acts I grow;
   I doubt my passing words, however brief;
   I catch his glances feeling like a thief.
Perchance he wonders why I shun him so, –
It would be strange indeed if he should know
   I love him, love him, love him past belief!
   JOHN GAMBRIL NICHOLSON (1866-1931)

I feel a-weeping and I cried, 'Sweet youth,
Tell me why, sad and sighing, thou dost rove
These pleasant realms? I pray thee speak me sooth
What is thy name?' He said, 'My name is Love.'
Then straight the first did turn himself to me
And cried, 'He lieth, for his name is Shame,
But I am Love, and I was wont to be
Alone in this fair garden, till he came
Unasked by night; I am true Love, I fill
The hearts of boy and girl with mutual flame.'
Then sighing said the other, 'Have thy will,
I am the Love that dare not speak its name.'
   LORD ALFRED DOUGLAS (1870-1945)

What in God's name does one call this sensibility if it be not love? ... This incredible feeling of sisterhood.
   DOROTHY THOMPSON (1894-1961)

Love of man for woman waxes and wanes.
Love of brother for brother
is as steadfast as the stars.
  HERBERT BRENON, 1926
  Opening title of *Beau Geste*

I caught sight of a splendid Misses. She had handkerchiefs
and kisses. She had eyes and yellow shoes she had
everything to choose and she chose me. In passing through
France she wore a Chinese hat and so did I. In looking at
the sun she read a map. And so did I. In eating fish and
pork she just grew fat. And so did I. In loving a blue sea she
had a pain. And so did I. In loving me she of necessity
thought first. And so did I. How prettily we swim. Not in
water. Not on land. But in love.
  GERTRUDE STEIN (1874-1946)
  about Alice B. Toklas

We that were friends tonight have found
  A fear, a secret, and a shame:
I am on fire with that soft sound
  You make, in uttering my name.

Forgive a young and boastful man
  Whom dreams delight and passions please,
And love me as great women can
  Who have no children at their knees.
  JAMES ELROY FLECKER (1884-1915)

116

Oh! I want to put my arms around you, I ache to hold you close. Your ring is a great comfort. I look at it & think she does love me or I wouldn't be wearing it.

ELEANOR ROOSEVELT (1884-1962)

letter to her lover, Lorena Hickock

Long-term relationships between two males are notably few.

ALFRED KINSEY (1894-1956)

Saturday night I at last was taken into the arms of love again! Seldom have I had such affection offered me. An athlete – very strong – 20 only – dark-haired – distantly Bohemian. I hope it will last a while – I deserve a little kindness and he *was* so kind!

HART CRANE (1899-1932)

letter to his friend, Wilbur Underwood

The actual facts are so very simple. I love you. You love me. You love Otto. I love Otto. Otto loves you. Otto loves me.

NOEL COWARD (1899-1973)

Leo, in *Design for Living*, to his roommate and friend, Gilda

Marriage! What a strange word to be applied to two men! Can't you hear the hell-hounds of society baying full pursuit behind us? But that's just the point. We are beyond society. We've said thank you very much, and stepped outside and closed the door.

FRANCIS OTTO MATTHIESSEN (1902-50)

The only abnormality is the incapacity to love.
    ANAÏS NIN (1903-77)

If equal affection cannot be,
Let the more loving one be me.
    W.H. AUDEN (1907-73)

I could not make love to boys without loving them.
    JEAN GENET (1910-86)

Claire, if I speak of the smell of garrets, it is for memory's sake. And of the twin beds where two sisters fall asleep, dreaming of one another.
    JEAN GENET (1910-86)
    Solange to Claire, in *The Maids*

Why I think that's the most contemptible thing you could do – marry a woman and use her as a cloak to cover what you are.
    MAE WEST, 1927
    Grayson, in *The Drag*

I have frequently given my best sexual performance with people I didn't love, in fact rather despised. I have fucked the arses off ageing queens quite easily, but found a beautiful young boy often too difficult to come, because I loved him too much.
    JOE ORTON (1933-67)

A multitude of men who love only men marry and become fathers. Fed to satiety with the overflowing bounty of woman in a single wife, they don't so much as lay a hand on another woman. Among the world's devoted husbands men of this kind are not few. If they have children, they become more mother than father to them. Some women prefer a peaceful life, and such men.

YUKIO MISHIMA (1925-70)
Shunsuke, in *Thirst for Love*

Too many people, both straight and gay, see gay relationships as sad, necessarily transient sadomasochistic parodies of heterosexual marriage which cause nothing but unhappiness to the parties involved. This is simply not true ... Same-sex relationships are no more problematic but no easier than any other human relationships. They are in many ways the same and in several ways different from heterosexual relationships but in themselves are no less possible or worthwhile.

CHRISTOPHER LARKIN, 1973

[He] needed love. That it was homosexual love was, in my opinion, of no importance. It was the only variety available and the need was crucial.

So we became lovers.

JAMES BLAKE, 1970
regarding his experience as chapel organist in a prison

All heterosexual relationships are corrupted by the imbalance of power between men and women.

JANIS KELLY, 1972

Today, after many years of a successful marriage, with a happy home and with children, and with a firm bond of friendship that has developed with a man who has been an inspiring person in my life, I sit down to relate what it means to be a homosexual. This is not the thinking of a bitter and unhappy person. It is the accumulated experience and outlook of one who has been through the struggle with himself and with society.

DONALD WEBSTER CORY, 1980s

One of the most frequent myths created by both the heterosexual and gay worlds is that gay lovers don't remain together. It is shocking how many young gay men believe this to be true.

CHARLES SILVERSTEIN, 1981

Belonging is a form of identification. One may identify as a lesbian, but lesbianism has little reclaimed history and no traditions. There are no celebrations to mark the stages in the life of a lesbian, her initiation or her union with another, no coming-of-age rituals, weddings, or lesbian gatherings at the birth of a child. Even at her death, a lesbian's life-long commitment to another woman may be contested or made invisible by omission.

SAVINE TEUBAL, 1982

I am so *bored* with normal-looking people, whether they're gay or not. And besides being boring, it's a big lie to tell all those people out there that what we want is the same lifestyle as theirs, the same suburb, the same house; to adopt children and live like *them*. It's just a big lie. It's the way we dress ourselves up to make ourselves more comfortable with our straight friends.

RICHARD BENNER, 1979

I have seen lesbian plums which cling to each other
in the tightest of monogamous love
and I have watched lesbian pumpkins
declare the whole patch their playground.
  MARTHA COURTOT, 1984

No scientific differentiation has ever been proposed, nor is
it easy to conceive of an experiment which might be
performed to determine whether one person's love for
another was friendly or erotic. From a phenomenological
point of view, it seems likely that 'friendship' and 'love' are
simply different points on a scale measuring a constellation
of psychological and physiological responses to other
humans.
  JOHN BOSWELL, 1980

Spinsterhood is a Gay office that has passed through the
transition of women's central and controlling position in
societies to the patriarchal systems of today's world.
Because the office always allows women to avoid marriage
and establish or maintain an independent economic base, it
has been of primary importance to the survival of women's
freedom, hope, and the ability to express ourselves outside
of family life.
  JUDITH GRAHN, 1984

Don't be 100 percent certain about the differences between
a Trick, a Number, a Thing, a Relationship and a Lover.
Get them confused once in a while. Try occasionally to
have a Thing with a Lover or a Relationship with a Trick.
  TONY LANG, 1985

The primary difference between a heterosexual marriage and a homosexual relationship is that the law covers the operation of one and has nothing to do with the other.

MARK SENAK, 1985
vice chair AIDS Resource Center, Inc.

Visible gay couples are rare role models and should strive to present the best possible impression.

BRYAN MONTE, 1986

After all, straight people shouldn't have a monopoly on Bloomingdale's bridal registry. I'd love to have a few place settings of Fitz & Floyd china on my breakfront.

CRAIG G. HARRIS, 1986

Nowhere is it said that he who lives alone cannot have a lover. There are perfectly logical and rational reasons for lovers to maintain separate residences. The reasons may be professional and they may be personal.

JOHN E. JONES, 1986

If you do have a hankering to be formally bonded, don't be ashamed. Go for it! Chart out a game plan, find that man of your dreams and claim him.

CRAIG G. HARRIS, 1986

In calling ourselves gay we say that love is central, and after the shame and guilt, and yes after the anger, love remains a word we can speak unabashed while others cringe at its too-telling power. We are the subjects of the power of love.

AARON SHURIN, 1987

Sure, a lot of gays who live in the mainstream have friends and family who care just as much about them. But there's something intangibly unique about the constant caring and loving that gays living in Community give to one another. It is a love that overcomes diverse backgrounds – a love that transcends disagreements. But most of all, it is a love that survives our ephemeral bonds to this planet.

RICHARD OSBORNE, 1988

Politics and the Law

If a man also lie with mankind, as he lieth with a woman, both of them have committed an abomination: they shall surely be put to death; their blood shall be upon them.

THE BIBLE
Leviticus 20:13 (725? BC)

[Homosexuality] is regarded as shameful by the Ionians and many others under foreign domination. It is shameful to barbarians because of their despotic government, just as philosophy and athletics are, since it is apparently not in the best interests of such rulers to have great ideas engendered in their subjects, or powerful friendships or physical unions, all of which love is particularly apt to produce ... Wherever, therefore, it has been established that it is shameful to be involved in homosexual relationships, this is due to evil on the part of the legislators, to despotism on the part of the rulers, and to cowardice on the part of the governed.

PLATO (427? BC-347 BC)

I know there are some people who call them shameless; but they are wrong. It is not immodesty that leads them to such pleasures, but daring, fortitude, and masculinity; the very virtues that they recognize and welcome in their lovers – which is proved by the fact that in after years they are the only men who show any real manliness in public life.

PLATO (427? BC-347 BC)

If then one could contrive that a state or an army should entirely consist of lovers and loved, it would be impossible for it to have a better organization than that which it would then enjoy through their avoidance of all dishonor and their mutual emulation; moreover, a handful of such men, fighting side by side, would defeat practically the whole world. A lover would rather be seen by all his comrades leaving his post or throwing away his arms than by his beloved; rather than that, he would prefer a thousand times to die.

PLATO (427? BC-347 BC)

Anyone who persuades a boy who has been either abducted by him or by his corrupt accomplices to submit to lewdness ... shall be punished with death; and if it is not accomplished, he shall be deported to some island. Their corrupted accomplices shall suffer the extreme penalty.

JUSTINIAN I (483-565?)

What we are is a crime, if it is a crime to love,
For the God who made me live made me love.

BAUDRI OF BOURGUEIL (1046-1130)

125

'The people with power and position in the world –
The very censors who decide what is sin and what is
   allowed –
These men are not immune to the soft thighs of a boy.'
   MEDIEVAL POET, c. 1120
   Ganymede, in *Ganymede and Helen*

The church allows a hermaphrodite – that is, someone with
the organs of both sexes, capable of either active or passive
functions – to use the organ by which [s]he is most aroused
or the one to which [s]he is more susceptible.

Of [s]he is more active, [s]he may wed as a man, but if
[s]he is more passive, [s]he may marry as a woman. If,
however, [s]he should fail with one organ, the use of the
other can never be permitted, but s[h]e must be perpetually
celibate to avoid any similarity to the role inversion of
sodomy, which is detested by God.
   PETER CANTOR (1150?-92)

Go where we will, at ev'ry time and place,
Sodom confronts, and stares us in the face;
They ply in public at our very doors
And take the bread from much more honest Whores.
Those who are mean high Paramours secure,
And the rich guilty screen the guilty poor;
The Sin too proud to feel from Reason awe,
And Those, who practise it, too great for Law.
   CHARLES CHURCHILL (1731-64)

Paederasty became the crime of those to whom no crime could be imputed.
    EDWARD GIBBON (1737-94)
    Decline and Fall of the Roman Empire
    commenting on the persecutions of homosexuals
    during the reign of Justinian

[Homosexuality] is a crime, if a crime it is to be called, that produces no misery in Society.
    JEREMY BENTHAM (1748-1832)
    Nonconformity

What would have become of Aristides, Solon, Themistocles, Harmodius and Aristogiton, Xenophon, Cato, Socrates, Titus – the delight of Mankind, Cicero, Pliny, Trajan, Hadrian &c., &c. – these idols of their Country and ornaments of human Nature? They would have *perished on your Gibbets.*
    JEREMY BENTHAM (1748-1832)

I have been hunted down and persecuted these many years … No truce, no respite have I experienced since the first licence was taken out … for shooting at me.
    WILLIAM BECKFORD (1760-1844)
    an accused homosexual, enduring ostracism and exile

All the forces in the world are not so powerful as an idea whose time has come.
    VICTOR HUGO (1802-85)
    motto displayed on the wall in Harvey Milk's office

From native England, that endured too long
The ceaseless burden of his impious song;
His mad career of crimes and follies run,
And gray in vice, when life was scarce begun;
He goes, in foreign lands prepared to find
A life more suited to his guilty mind;
Where other climes new pleasures may supply
For that pall'd taste, and that unhallow'd eye.

LONDON NEWSPAPER, 1816
on the exile of Byron

Love, love, clandestine love, was still my dream.
Methought there must be yet some people found,
Where cupid's wings were free, his hands unbound
Where law had no erotic statutes framed,
Nor gibbets stood to fright the unreclaimed.

ENGLISH POET, 1833
from *Don Leon*, a purported autobiographical poem of
Byron's life

There have of course been, in all ages, thousands and
thousands of women who have not felt that particular sort
of romance and attraction toward men, but only to their
own kind; and in all ages there have been thousands and
thousands of men similarly constituted in the reverse way;
but they have been, by the majority, little understood and
recognized. Now however it is coming to be seen that they
also – both classes – have their part to play in the world.

EDWARD CARPENTER (1844-1929)

It is indeed a burning shame that there should be one law
for men and another law for women. I think there should
be no law for anybody.

OSCAR WILDE (1854-1900)

To be overtly homosexual, in a culture that denigrates and hates homosexuality, is to be political.
MICHAEL BRONSKI (1854-1900)

You've heard of my case? Don't distress youself. All is well. The working classes are with me ... to a boy.
OSCAR WILDE (1854-1900)
to Charles Goodhart, an actor friend

It is a great injustice to persecute homosexuality as a crime, and cruelty too.
SIGMUND FREUD (1856-1939)

In spite of all present-day clamour about ... different rights for different individualities, there is only one law that governs mankind ... It is in opposition to that law ... that we forbid the homosexualist to carry on his practices whilst we allow the heterosexualist full play ... The only logical ... treatment for sexual inverts would be to allow them to seek and obtain what they require when they can, that is to say, among other inverts.
OTTO WEININGER, 1920s
pioneer sexologist

It will probably be difficult to convince the generation succeeding ours that, when this country was at its zenith of her commercial prosperity, it was improper to utter the word homosexuality, prurient to admit its existence and pornographic to discuss the subject.
JOSEPH COLLINS (1866-1950)

We had a grand time – The police were perfectly lovely to us – weren't they, girls? ... Perfectly lovely. Why the minute I walked into jail, the captain said – Well, Kate, what kind of a cell would you like to have? And I said – Oh, any kind will do, Captain, just so it has a couple of peep-holes in it. I crave fresh air.

> MAE WEST, 1927
> Kitchen Kate, a transvestite from *The Drag*

The port's on the sideboard, Herbert, and remember it's adultery just the same.

> MAUD BEERBOHM TREE (1864-1937)
> on finding her husband, actor Sir Herbert Beerbohm
> Tree, dining intimately at home with a handsome
> young actor

> MILITARY MAN: Tell me, Mr Strachey, what would you
> do if you saw a German soldier attempting to rape
> your sister?
> STRACHEY: I should try and come between them.
> LYTTON STRACHEY (1880-1932)

With us love is just as punishable as murder or robbery.

> MARGARET ANDERSON (1886-1973)

Won't you stop this continued heckling about homosexuals and let us get on with the main work of finding Communists?

> MILLARD TYDINGS (1890-1961)
> at a meeting of the US Senate

You can't hardly separate homosexuals from subversives. Mind you, I don't say every homosexual is a subversive, and I don't say every subversive is a homosexual. But a man of low morality is a menace in the government, whatever he is, and they are all tied up together.

> KENNETH WHERRY (1892-1951)

I'm very militant, you know, in a quiet way.
CHRISTOPHER ISHERWOOD (1904-86)

Generally, a fascist regime is against homosexuals. Only don't forget that in Hitler's regime the opposite was also true. The Hitler Jugend were very often homosexuals or in any case leaned toward homosexuality. So there were these two aspects. The same ambiguity exists in all examples of fascism, every time the masses are controlled, unified, or given to military exercise.
JEAN-PAUL SARTRE (1905-80)

Sir, I'll be happy to do this investigation for you but you'll have to know that the first name on the list will be mine ... I think the General should be aware that among those women are the most highly decorated women in the war.
SERGEANT JOHNNIE PHELPS, 1940s
her reply to General Eisenhower concerning his request that she seek out and uncover any lesbians in her WAC battalion

Perhaps as dangerous as the actual Communists are the sexual perverts who have infiltrated our Government in recent years. The State Department has confessed that it has had to fire ninety-one of these. It is the talk of Washington and of the Washington correspondents corps.
GUY GEORGE GABRIELSON
American Republican National Chairman, 1950

[H. Edgar Hoover is a] killer fruit.
TRUMAN CAPOTE (1924-84)

You're not given power, you have to take it.
HARVEY MILK (1930-78)

Whatever happens, I shall never be alone. I shall always have a boy, a railway fare, or a revolution.
STEPHEN SPENDER, 1955

You won't find a policeman around here; they're all over on the west side of the park chasing fairies down from trees or out of the bushes. That's all they do. That's their function.
EDWARD ALBEE, 1959
Jerry, in *The Zoo Story*

I do not see the NAACP and CORE worrying about which chromosome and gene produces black skin or about the possibility of bleaching the Negro. I do not see any great interest on the part of the B'nai B'rith Anti-Defamation League in the possibility of solving problems of anti-Semitism by converting Jews to Christianity.

In all of these minority groups, we are interested in obtaining rights for our respective minorities as Negroes, as Jews, and as homosexuals. Why we are Negroes, Jews, or homosexuals is totally irrelevant, and whether we can be changed to whites, Christians, or heterosexuals is equally irrelevant.
FRANK KAMENY
founder of the Washington Mattachine Society,
1960s

In the Forties the Bomb dropped. In the Forties the entire planet was threatened biologically. In the Forties there was a recovery from a total breakdown of all morality in the concentration camps. For those of us who were homosexual, it was the realization of, why are we being intimidated by a bunch of jerks who don't know anything about life? Who were they to tell us what to feel and how we're supposed to behave?

ALLEN GINSBERG, 1960s

Every person who commits any of the following acts shall be guilty of disorderly conduct, a misdemeanor: (a) Who solicits anyone to engage in or who in any public place or in any place open to the public or exposed to public view engages in lewd or dissolute conduct ... (d) Who loiters in or about any toilet open to the public for the purpose of engaging in or soliciting any lewd or lascivious or any unlawful act.

CALIFORNIA PENAL CODE SECTION 647, 1961

A case could be made, let us say, for removing criminal sanctions against homosexuality between consenting adults. But the modernists want to go further and, in effect, remove the moral sanctions against such behavior; and that is something else again. All that is good is not embodied in the law; and all that is evil is not proscribed by the law. A well-disciplined society needs few laws; but it needs strong mores.

WILLIAM F. BUCKLEY JR, 1966

Oral copulation by and between two women constitutes 'unnatural carnal copulation' within the statue proscribing such conduct.

Louisiana Supreme Court ruling, 1967

Sodomy (a legal term for anal intercourse) is a felony crime in most states, punishable by long prison terms. The name is derived from the Biblical city destroyed because of its 'wickedness'. But what were they doing in Gomorrah?
DR EUGENE SCHOENFELD, 1968

Judges realize that putting a homosexual into prison is like trying to cure obesity by incarceration in a candy shop.
MARTIN HOFFMAN, 1968

I'm all for bringing back the birch, but only between consenting adults.
GORE VIDAL, 1969

Cheers would go up as favorites would emerge from the door, strike a pose, and swish by the detective with a 'Hello there, fella.' The stars were in their element. Wrists were limp, hair was primped, and reactions to the applause were classic. 'I gave them the gay power bit and they loved it, girls.'
THE VILLAGE VOICE, 1969
on the police raiding of the Stonewall dance bar in Greenwich Village, 27 June 1969

The gay lib movement should consolidate with the other lib movements – the women's lib movement, and particularly with the revolutionary movements which are nonviolent – and become a single thrust toward emancipation in America.
TENNESSEE WILLIAMS, 1970s

We have to define for ourselves a new pluralistic, rolefree social structure. It must contain both the freedom and the physical space for people to live alone, live together for a

134

while, live together for a long time, either as couples or in large numbers; and the ability to flow easily from one of these states to another as our needs change.

CARL WITTMAN, 1972

We are the negation of heterosexuality and of the nuclear family structure, and as such we have been driven from our jobs, our families, our education, and sometimes from life itself.

KARLA JAY, 1972

A Lesbian is a woman whose primary erotic, psychological, emotional and social interest is in a member of her own sex, even though that interest may not be overtly expressed ... Like her heterosexual sister, the Lesbian has been downtrodden, but doubly so: first because she is a woman, and second, because she is a Lesbian.

DEL MARTIN AND PHYLLIS LYON, 1972

They kept us locked up for six months. For six months I went through every book in the library. I knitted doilies, I went through four bookkeeping courses. I was by myself in a cell maybe a yard wide and a yard deep. No toilets. We had a shit pail with disinfectant in it. We constructed our own toilet seats from our little pails, which we took out and emptied twice a day, then filled up with disinfectant again. They loved us so much they put the entire TB ward on the deck right below us, because it didn't make any difference if the homosexuals and sexual perverts got TB.

GUY T. OLMSTEAD, 1973
American convict imprisoned for homosexual acts

The rights and dignity of homosexuals are not a controversial issue.
GAY ACTIVISTS ALLIANCE AND NATIONAL GAY TASK FORCE, 1973

Homosexuality is a worldwide economic fact.
WILLIAM S. BURROUGHS, 1973

Bisexuality is not so much a copout as a fearful compromise.
JILL JOHNSTON, 1973

Women who practise bisexuality today are simply leading highly privileged lives that do not challenge male power and that, in fact, undermine the feminist struggle.
LORETTA ULMSCHREIDER, 1974

At first, I thought gay liberation would mean freedom from sexual bondage, leaving your mate, the women's liberation stuff that comics make fun of. Later, I discovered that the most important part was finding yourself.
ARTHUR BELL, 1977

Demonstrations which define the homosexual as a unique minority defeat the very cause for which the homosexual strives – to be an integral part of society.
SHIRLEY WILLER,

As a minority, we homosexuals are therefore caught in a particularly vicious circle. On the one hand, the shame of belonging and the social punishment of acknowledgement are so great that pretense is almost universal; on the other hand, only a leadership that would acknowledge [us] would be able to break down the barriers of shame and resultant discrimination.

DONALD WEBSTER CORY, 1980s

I am suggesting that heterosexuality, like motherhood, needs to be recognized and studied as a political institution – even, or especially, by those individuals who feel they are, in their personal experience, the precursors of a new social relation between the sexes.

ADRIENNE RICH, 1980s

In 1948, I went to a gay party and we started talking about forming a 'Bachelors for Wallace' [organization] … We would have a plank, and educate people about who we were, about how we weren't bad people; we would end entrapment, and begin a whole new movement for the gay peoples. I was so excited, I went home and wrote it all up. When I called them the next day, they all said, 'Forget it, honey'; it was the beer.

HARRY HAY, 1980s

We always find ourselves in the position of having to play civil libertarian to a bunch of bigots who want their constitutional right to express their hatred of us.

RONALD GOLD, 1980

Lesbian and gay rights will continue to be eroded unless the silence that usually greets these actions is broken.

ELEANOR COOPER AND JIM LEVIN
Coalition for Lesbian and Gay Rights, 1981

Most feminists probably don't give a tiny damn about the sex that gay men have together as long as in their lives they actively oppose the oppression of all women.

SALLY M. GEARHART, 1982

The core of feminism is choice. All women and men are to have the freedom to choose whatever kind of lives they wish in a feminist society. They will not be constrained by gender expectations to choose a career, a particular lifestyle, or only one kind of sexuality. It was this vision of freedom that attracted me to feminism in the first place. I was a lesbian before I was a feminist, and a fag hag before I was aware of either. Now I am a revolting fag hag. Seeing the situation in the feminist community has made me revolt and proclaim my complete lack of sympathy for this parody of feminism.

LINDA FRANKEL, 1982

As women and as lesbians we have learned to reclaim names like dyke, bitch, manhater, golddigger, shrew, harpy, whore, cunt, amazon; (even) lesbian, even *woman* had first to be reclaimed from a place of squeamishness.

MELANIE KAY, 1982

The simple, obvious thing would have been to go to the senior prom with a girl. But that would have been a lie – a lie to myself, to the girl, and to all the other students. What I wanted to do was to take a male date.

AARON FRICKE, 1982
    at seventeen he stood up to community and school
    authorities and won their permission to bring a male
    date to his high school prom

'When are you going to make your mother
    twice a grandma?'
No way. My womb, like my fist,
    is clenched aginst the world.
    MARTHA SHELLEY, 1982

To choose only other lesbians means to deny the centuries of mothers, the centuries of slaves behind her, in their particular prisons, forming their particular prides, leaving inside of the daughters a particular way. But to choose your mother as well as other lesbians renders all lesbians vulnerable to the attacks of men as the mothers transmit them, to the softer ties of false safety, the smell of holiday cooking, the access to the material world the mother woos with, bringing her daughter back home to the dungeon.
    ELANA DYKEWOMON, 1982

I don't know anyone who has a lower opinion of the attitudes that people have toward gay people than Harvey Milk had. He assumed that the most liberal people in our society despise gay people. But he always acted as though that were not true.
    REVD HARRY BRITT, 1982

Homosexuals are usually too self-directed to turn toward politics.
    NED ROREM, 1982

It is the same American mistake. To believe that having the same understanding, the same conclusion from the same facts, makes us therefore the same. It is antiseparatism to believe that in order to have a motion, it must all be the same motion, that all the words of the new language must come from the same root; it is mindless melting pot politics, to give away what has made you, to come forward pretending you are a blank slate.

ELANA DYKEWOMON, 1982

There is less and less doubt that the women's movement is perfectly willing to bully gay men over issues of male sexual expression.

JOHN PRESTON, 1983

In 1834, Alabama Senator William Rufus De Vane King (a fifty-seven-year-old bachelor) met Pennsylvania Senator James Buchanan, and the two were inseparable until King's appointment as US minister to France. Their intimate relationship caused barbed comments in Washington. Andrew Jackson called King 'Miss Nancy' ... Aaron Brown (in 1844, in a private letter) called King Buchanan's 'better half', referred, jestingly to King and Buchanan's 'divorce', and referred to King as 'she', 'her', and 'Aunt Fancy'; King refers to his 'communion' with Buchanan in a note of 1844.

JONATHAN KATZ, 1983

I came here today to ask that this nation with all its resources and compassion not let my epitaph read he died of red tape.

ROGER LYON, 1983
quoted on the quilt panel commemorating his death
from AIDS

One must again fall back on the fact that gay politics still rely on the dynamic of failure, still count on being rebuked as a means to mobilize the great unwashed apathetic folk who merely need the right incentive to get involved. Behind this is a fantasy that one day gays, charged by some apocalyptic defeat, will march by the millions, shoulder to shoulder, through the streets of the nation. It is time to point out that this has nothing to do with politics.

LARRY BUSH, 1983

They call Ronald Reagan the great communicator. Well, any man that can call a nuclear missile 'Peacemaker' is free to call his son 'Butch'.

TOM AMMIANO, 1984

The first gay meeting which grew into the gay liberation movement was held in 1950 in someone's apartment in Los Angeles, and the door was locked and the blinds were drawn and there was a lookout posted because they thought it was illegal to talk about homosexuality.

BARBARA GITTINGS
American director of the Gay Task Force, American Library Association, 1985

We have cooperated for a very long time in the maintenance of our own invisibility. And now the party is over.

VITO RUSSO, 1985

Don't make derisive remarks about the lesbians who are marching with you.

TONY LANG, 1985

I simply refuse to give up the party of Lincoln to the bigots ... I know that most Republicans don't have a very good track record on gay rights, but I believe that someday the

Republican party will come around, absolutely. Otherwise, what's the alternative? To put all our eggs in one basket?

LEONARD MATLOVICH

American Air Force sergeant discharged for being gay, 1988

We hold that the Army's regulations violate the constitutional guarantee of equal protection of the laws because they discriminate against persons of homosexual orientation.

APPEALS PANEL, US COURT, 1988

Ironically, according to some estimates, as many as 20 to 25 percent of the officers in the San Francisco Police Department are gay men or lesbians.

CHARLES LINEBARGER, 1988

Are you playing God and judging that this group is morally wrong and should not be protected? And if you are making that judgement, why don't you stand up in public to the people of this state to see if they agree with you?

MARIO CUOMO, 1988

Rare are reports of straight people arrested in lovers' lanes, but gay men are frequently hauled in. Some undercover cops go to great lengths to entice gay men into taking the bait. Officers have been known to smile and wink and rub their groins. Their activity at times borders on entrapment.

DAVE WALTER, 1988

This just goes to prove my long-standing theory: Some straight men – or should I say semi-straight men or hoping-and-praying-they're-straight men – just can't seem to get enough of anything gay. They're fascinated. Entranced. Some would say obsessed. No excuse is too flimsy.

MARGERY EAGAN, 1988

regarding the police spying on gay groups

Sexual activities in places that are truly public are crimes and should legitimately be crimes.

TOM STODDARD, 1988

The pressures of growing up gay, developing a gay persona in a straight society, and then acclimating one's lifestyle comfortably into society makes a person particularly sensitive to undercurrents in social issues. Due to this cultural trait, the gay community will become an influential segment of the population and will be recognized as economically and politically powerful.

IAN LYNCH, 1988

I have a duty, and I intend to fulfill that duty, and my duty is to assist people who are gay or lesbian or who have AIDS to be free of discrimination. I will perform that duty, and I'm not going to look back to see how many people wished I had or wished I hadn't, because my clients are very happy that they have someone to assist them, and they are my main concern.

GLORIA ALLRED, 1988

America is not a blanket, woven from one thread, one color, one cloth. [We] must build a quilt together ... Blacks and Hispanics, when we fight for civil rights, we are right – but our patch isn't big enough. Gays and lesbians, when you fight against discrimination and for a cure for AIDS, you are right – but your patch isn't big enough. Conservatives and progressives, when you fight for what you believe, you are right – but your patch isn't big enough ... But when we bring the patches together, we make a quilt ... [Then] we, the people, always win.

REVD JESSE JACKSON, 1988

God Save the Queens.

PROTEST PLACARD SLOGAN, 1988

at demonstrations in Holland during Queen Elizabeth II's state visit, following the institution of the new Section 28

Call us by name.

TERJE ANDERSON, 1988

regarding the Democratic platform's unwillingness to mention gay rights issues

The US Olympics Committee singled out the Gay Olympics with a lawsuit prohibiting the use of the word 'Olympics'. They didn't sue the Armenian Olympics, the Black Olympics, the Chinese Olympics. They only sued the Gay Olympics. I know that the USOC claims that it was a question of trademark law, not homophobia. But let me tell you this: Anyone who believes that must think that Rosa Parks's struggle to sit where she wanted on a Montgomery bus was really about transit policy.

ART AGNOS, 1988

Mayor of San Francisco

I didn't start the sexual liberation movement, but I was a part of it when it was ready to start.

CHRISTINE JORGENSEN (1927-89)
pioneer transsexual

It was inevitable that outrageousness exploded with the beginnings of gay liberation. Hooray for sassy risk and silly experiment and anarchic joy!

JAMES BROUGHTON, 1987

Every stich in Dr Tom Waddell's quilt is a stitch of rage – for the insensitivity of the present administration to act against this epidemic, for the misunderstanding of some, but most of all to the United States Supreme Court for their denial of the use of the word 'Olympic' associated with games Dr Waddell founded.

Shame on you!

Shame on you, not only for the denial of the use of the word 'Olympic', but also shame on you that my quilt for Dr Thomas Waddell doesn't have love in every stitch.

A. CHRISTOPHER PRIESTLY, 1988
note accompanying quilt panel to NAMES Project
honoring Dr Tom Waddell, Olympic decathlete and
founder of the Gay 'Olympics'

[We] have allowed our governors to divide the population into two teams. [One] is good, godly, straight; the other is evil, sick, vicious.

GORE VIDAL, 1988

Sure, I would fight for access to Tompkins Square Park. I've met some of my most gratifying sexual partners there. In fact I've *had* some of my most gratifying sexual experiences there.

CLIFFORD SCHWARTZ, 1988

I am frustrated with those who call me a victim, stripping me of both my personal and political power. I am not a victim. I cannot think of myself as a victim and survive. I am a person with AIDS.

KEITH GANN, 1988

Psychology

[The homosexual] disposition occurs in some people naturally ... When nature is responsible, no one would call such persons immoral, any more than they would women because they are passive in intercourse rather than active ... And whether the individual so disposed conquers or yields to it is not properly a moral issue.

ARISTOTLE (384 BC-322 BC)

It certainly does not seem impossible to suppose that as the ordinary love has a special function in the propagation of the race, so the other has its special function in social and heroic work and in the generation not of bodily children but of those children of the mind – the philosophical conceptions and ideals which transform our lives and those of society.

EDWARD CARPENTER (1844-1929)

Indulgent male inverts like pleasant, artistic things, and nearly all of them are fond of music. They also like praise and admiration. They are poor whistlers. Their favorite color is green ... Active male homosexuals are not prone to make sacrifices, personal or social, as was observed in the analysis of war neuroses. Some aggressive homosexual women wear male attire, and are often very proficient in business, sports, etc. The passive ones are of the clinging type, who like to kiss other girls.

JOHN F.W. MEAGHER, 1929

Every impulse that we strive to strangle broods in the mind and poisons us.

OSCAR WILDE (1854-1900)

It has been said that the great events of the world take place in the brain. It is in the brain, and the brain only, that the great sins of the world take place.

OSCAR WILDE (1854-1900)
The Picture of Dorian Gray

Homosexuality is assuredly no advantage, but it is nothing to be ashamed of, no vice, no degradation, it cannot be classified as an illness.

SIGMUND FREUD (1856-1939)

To be 'cured' against one's will and cured of states which we may not regard as disease is to be put on a level with those who have not yet reached the age of reason.

C.S. LEWIS (1898-1963)

All persons originally are bisexual in their predisposition. There are no exceptions.

WILHELM STEKEL (1868-1940)

The homosexual is often a man of considerable intellect and ability. It is found that the cycle of these individuals' homosexual desires follows the cycle closely patterned to the menstrual period of women. There may be three or four days in each month that the homosexual's instincts break down and drive the individual into abnormal fields of sexual practice. Under large doses of sedatives during this sensitive cycle, he may escape such acts.

ARTHUR LEWIS MILLER, 1950

Homosexuality as a clinical entity does not exist. It forms are as varied as are those of heterosexuality.

EVELYN HOOKER, 1957

There seems to be no valid evidence to show that homosexuality, per se, is a sickness. In view of the absence of such valid evidence, the simple fact that the suggestion of sickness has been made is no reason for entertaining it seriously, or for abandoning the view that homosexuality is not a sickness, but merely a liking or preference similar to and fully on a part with heterosexuality. Accordingly, I take the position unequivocally that, until and unless valid, positive evidence shows otherwise, homosexuality, per se, is neither a sickness, a defect, a disturbance, a neurosis, a psychosis, not a malfunction of any sort.

FRANK KAMENY, 1965

Virtually all the literature on homosexuality is marred by the failure of its authors to take account of the fact that heterosexuality is just as much a problematic situation for the student of human behavior as is homosexuality. The only reason it does not seem to us a problem is because we take its existence for granted.

MARTIN HOFFMAN, 1968

There is no definition of 'homosexual' or 'homosexuality' which is going to be agreed to by 100 percent of the scientists working in this field.

MARTIN HOFFMAN, 1968

Bachelor baboons who have restricted opportunities for contact with females sometimes strike up homosexual friendships, and for a time a masculine pair remains constantly together. Immature males often join full-grown bachelors and engage in sexual activity. Prepuberal and adolescent males show a wide range of sex responses. They display the feminine sexual presentation, masturbate, and mount one another. They also mount and are mounted by adult members of their own sex. And they engage in manual, oral, and olfactory genital examination with other males of their own age.

C.S. FORD AND F.A. BEACH, 1970

The branch of medicine we are most concerned with is psychiatry. The American medical profession is oblivious to the needs of oppressed people, and psychiatrists are clearly hostile to homosexuality.

CHICAGO GAY LIBERATION FOR THE REVOLUTIONARY
PEOPLE'S CONSTITUTIONAL CONVENTION
working paper, 1970

I conceive of two distinct categories – heterosexual and homosexual ... The two categories are ... mutually exclusive and cannot be placed on the same continuum ... A man is homosexual if his behavior is homosexual. Self-identification is not relevant.

IRVING BIEBER, 1971

You ask about what we were interested in finding out about homosexuality. Nothing vastly different than what we're looking for in heterosexuality. What makes it happen? I think when you find the answer to one, you find the answer to the other.

VIRGINIA JOHNSON, 1972

Homosexuality doesn't change people's basic traits. Especially their need to be wanted and loved.

DAVID REUBEN, 1972

Homosexuality – like heterosexuality – becomes self-fulfilling.

PEPPER SCHWARTZ AND PHILIP BLUMSTEIN, 1973

[My grandmother] had just begun practising on her own, under Freud's supervision, in Vienna, and she took on a patient who was a Lesbian. My grandmother was disturbed because, although the analysis finally concluded success-fully – the woman could deal with various problems in her life – she was still as Lesbian. My grandmother was rather worried about what Freud would say about this turn of events. When she next saw Freud the first thing he said was, 'Congratulations on your great success with Miss X.' My grandmother, startled, said, 'But she's still a Lesbian.' To which Freud replied, 'What does it matter as long as she's happy?'

NICHOLAS DEUTSCH, 1974
gay activist and grandson of Helene Deutsch,
psychoanalyst

Admittedly homosexuals can be conditioned to react sexually to a woman, or to an old boot for that matter. In fact both homo- and heterosexual experimental subjects *have been* conditioned to react sexually to a boot – to an old boot. You can save a lot of money that way.

WILLIAM S. BURROUGHS, 1978

The game [football] is a way of allowing us to have physical contact with other men ... The truth hurts, and I think I've struck a nerve. Face it, there's got to be more to football than a nice way to spend Saturday afternoon. Eighty thousand people don't turn out for the Roller Derby.

ALAN DUNDES, 1978

Homosexuality cannot be classed as a perversion on phenomenological grounds. Nothing rules out the full range of interpersonal perceptions between persons of the same sex.

THOMAS NAGEL, 1979

The majority of homosexuals, male and female, are not degenerates ... There are many persons who indulge in unnatural sexual relations who are not homosexuals. They are the real degenerates. There are many potential and active homosexuals whose intercourse with persons of their own sex is confined to emotional and intellectual contact, to establishing romantic friendship ... There are others in which interecourse is physical as well. The rank and file considers them degenerates.

JOSEPH COLLINS (1866-1950)

It's hard for young people today to imagine that as little as 20 years ago a hundred gay people were sitting around arguing over whether or not they should say that they weren't mentally ill.

CRAIG RODWELL, 1982
opened American's first gay bookstore

Since many sex therapy techniques include the use of either commercial or educational erotica, it is problematic, although not surprising, that many lesbian clients find such male-created images either degrading or uninteresting.

LAURA S. BROWN, 1986

The meeting of two personalities is like the contact of two chemical substances: if there is any reaction, both are transformed.

CARL GUSTAV JUNG (1875-1961)

Religion

Zeus, to steal boy Ganymede,
  And eagle's form put on;
And when he wanted the lady Leda
  He turned into a swan.

Now some like girls, and some like boys;
  But the moral's plain to see:
If both are good enough for Zeus,
  They're good enough for me.

GREEK POET

Those very people who have been nourished by godly doctrine, who instruct others in what they ought not to do, who have heard the Scriptures brought down from heaven, these do not consort with prostitutes as fearlessly as they do with young men.

The fathers of the young men take this in silence: they do not try to sequester their sons, nor do they seek any remedy for this evil.

None is ashamed, no one blushes, but, rather, they take pride in their little game; the chaste seem to be the odd ones, and the disapproving the ones in error.

ST JOHN CHRYSOSTOM (347-407)

Scorch, God, with a blow of your thunderbolt, the
    enemy of nature
Who wastes the labour of creation in the lap of a male.
    MEDIEVAL MONK, 1150?

I dwelt amonge the Sodomytes,
The Beniamytes, and Madyanytes,
And nowe the popysshe hypocrytes
Embrace me every where.
    JOHN BALE (1495-1563)
    Sodomismus, allegorical monk in a satirical anti-
    Catholic poem

St John the Evangelist was bedfellow to Christ.
    CHRISTOPHER MARLOWE (1564-93)

The Lord of Heaven send you a sweet and blithe
awakening, all kind of comfort in your sanctified bed, and
bless the fruits thereof, that I may have sweet Bedchamber
boys to play with me (and this is my daily prayer).
    KING JAMES I (1566-1625)

If it be sin to love a lovely lad, oh, then sin I.
    RICHARD BARNFIELD (1574-1627)

Come, my Lucasia, since we see
    That Miracles Men's faith do move,
By wonder and by prodigy
    To the dull angry world let's prove
    There's a Religion in our Love.
    KATHERINE PHILIPS (1631-64)

No David could woo his Jonathan more
Than our hearts have wooed each other.
How sweet 't would be, as true souls' friends,
To strive for the dearest blessing of all
From God, the greatest of all Friends.

    AAGJE DEKEN (1741-1804)
    from a poem to her friend, Maria Bavink

Jesus has on the whole field of sexual irregularity preserved an uninterrupted silence.

    JEREMY BENTHAM (1748-1832)
    Nonconformity

It is so true that a woman may be in love with a woman, and a man with a man. It is pleasant to be sure of it, because it is undoubtedly the same love that we shall feel when we are angels, when we ascend to the only fit place for the Mignons, where *sie fragen nicht nach Mann und Weib* ['they do not ask about man or woman'].

    MARGARET FULLER (1810-50)

I sought by love alone to go
Where God had writ an awful No;
Pride gave a guilty God to hell:
I have no pride: by love I fell.

Why this was done I cannot tell,
The mysterty is inscrutable:
I only know I pay the cost
With heart and soul and honour lost.

    SIR ROGER CASEMENT (1864-1916)

Is it too much to ask that I should be
  Allowed to prove
God's gift of infinite variety
  In human love?
  JOHN BARFORD (1886-1935)
  'Toleration'

Oh happy John! Such love can never end.
Closer than brothers are is friend to friend.
  You the divinity of it have proved,
  'Whom Jesus loved.'
  JOHN BARFORD (1886-1935)
  'Toleration'

Acknowledge us, oh God, before the whole world. Give us
also the right to our existence!
  RADCLYFFE HALL (1886-1943)
  Stephen Gordon, in *The Well of Loneliness*

How can you tell if you walk into a gay church?
Only half the congregation is kneeling.
  JOKE, 1970s

[Jesus Christ] never married, ran around with twelve guys,
and was even betrayed by a kiss from another guy.
  REVD TROY PERRY, 1972

The Lord Is My Shepherd and He Knows I'm Gay.
  REVD TROY PERRY, 1977
  American clergyman/gay religious rights activist
  the title of his autobiography

The range of behavior among those with a homosexual orientation is the same as among heterosexuals. Much homosexual behavior is sinful, but not simply by the fact that it is homosexual.

BISHOP MELVIN WHEATLEY, 1980s

Platonic friendships in ancient Athens were hardly chaste. Sexual experiences, even orgies, were supposed to bring about catharsis and purgation to both body and soul – the embrace of a male prostitute and a pretty boy led to salvation!

ROBERT BRAIN, 1977

Wystan [W.H. Auden] doesn't love God, he's just attracted to him.

MARC BLITZSTEIN (1905-64)

Do you feel it's right for priests to get married?
Only if they're in love.

JOKE, 1980s

I wouldn't recommend [that] a gay person join the Lutheran Church. I don't think it's possible for a gay person with integrity to stay within the church and not expect to fight.

JEFF JOHNSON, 1988

I live no longer in the usual world. I have forsaken the familiar. And soon, by an extreme gesture, I shall cease altogether to be human and become legend like Jesus, Buddha, Cybele.

GORE VIDAL, 1968
Myra Breckinridge, in *Myra Breckinridge*

Did you hear about the gay choirboy who choked on his first hymn?
JOKE, 1970s

Our ministry is one of public manifestation and habitual penetration. Our motto is 'Give up the guilt'. And we're going to do that through any form at our means – theater, dance, spiritual expression and therapy.
SISTERS OF PERPETUAL INDULGENCE, 1981
American performance group

According to Jewish Law, [lesbians] do not exist. I assure you, it's all very logical: we're not proscribed because we don't exist. If we existed, believe me, they'd be against us.
EVELYN TORTON BECK, 1982

In spite of my experience, I wouldn't say the convent is a hotbed of lesbianism. I think that many women have joined convents to escape sexuality, whether lesbian or heterosexual. A desire for obedience and dedication to God are often secondary to a need for celibacy and denial. The convent appears to be a haven, a world apart from the pressures and risks of this world. But such shelter exacts a price in self-denial that I was unwilling to pay. I wanted to affect this world, not remove myself from it.
JEAN O'LEARY, 1984
former nun

I am not saying that it is impossible to be a gay religious: I am saying that for me it was not possible. I could not keep the two worlds apart. I wanted to be part of the lesbian community, and I also wanted the awe and respect that

'Sister' evokes in the Catholic community. Not being true to either world was causing havoc within me. For me the bottom line was celibacy. Although I am more celibate now than I was in the convent, I am free to choose it, and that makes all the difference.

CHARLOTTE DOCLAR, 1984
former nun

My belief in a creator gave me my key; for as his creation, my desires and needs can be perceived as natural. Thus I live honestly as a gay person.

BENJAMIN MARCUS, 1984

Christians cannot allow homosexuals to have any more power or strength in this country.

CHRISTIANS FOR REAGAN, 1984
television advertisement

To be suddenly in a church where lesbians and gay men are accepted is an overwhelming experience. You're surprised to find those others because you thought you were the only gay Christian in the world.

REVD KAREN ZIEGLER, 1985

Homosexuals are the nicest people you can ever meet. They're kind, they're artistic, they are lonely people. You can't hate 'em to Jesus, you got to love 'em to Jesus.

LITTLE RICHARD, 1985

When I came out as a Lesbian, I traced my roots to Lesbos, claiming the Greek and Roman Goddesses as my own. Now I pray to darker Goddesses – Asherah, Mahalath, Amaterasu – whose names fill my mouth with joy.

SAPPHIRE, 1985

The bible-thumpers complain that erotica is to be blamed for nearly all of the sexual crimes in existence. Poppycock. Nothing could be farther from the truth. After a reader of gay male erotica becomes aroused, chances are minimal that he'll go out looking for sex on the streets.

SAMUEL M. STEWARD, 1985

There is no relationship more curious than the one that exists between gay people and organized religion, for they have long been among its greatest sufferers and saints.

MARK THOMPSON, 1987

The church remains today as closeted a community as any other major social institution, but with an unusually high proportion of homosexuals. Some sources within the church say that at least a third, if not more, of the hierarchy and clergy are gay.

REVD MALCOLM BOYD, 1987

The Holy Male is potential in every one of us. Men should be shown how to reach and to cherish the divine in one another. A quest for the ecstatic goes beyond cruising for a congenial sex object. It is not enough to get it up, get it on, and get it over with. In the urgency of our present situation we should look toward connecting imaginatively with the souls of our brothers.

JAMES BROUGHTON, 1987

Whereas heteros believe that spirituality requires the fervent denial of carnality ... for us gay folk the preprogrammed instinctual behaviors triggered by, and thus awakened by, our early sexual and sensual discoveries constitute for us the gateway to the growth of spirit in heart and mind.

HARRY HAY, 1987

Separation and Loneliness

For me, the vernal garlands bloom no more.
   Adieu! fond hope of mutual fire
With boy or girl in still-renewed desire!
   HORACE (65 BC-8 BC)

I wonder and cannot express my amazement
That my John has not hurried back to me,
Though he is forever promising that he will return.
Either the boy is sick, or he has forgotten me ... The boy
   is fickle like everything young.
   BAUDRI OF BOURGUEIL (1046-1130)

Sometimes I wish that I his pillow were,
So I might steale a kisse.
   RICHARD BARNFIELD (1574-1627)

I am sure my Bones would not rest in an English grave – or
my Clay mix with the earth of that Country: – I believe the
thought would drive me mad on my death-bed could I
suppose that any of my friends would be base enough to

163

convey my carcase back to your soil – I would not even feed
your worms – if I could help it.
LORD BYRON (1788-1824)
letter from Bologna after his banishment from
England for gay affairs

Is there even one other like me – distracted, his
friend, his lover, lost to him?
WALT WHITMAN (1819-92)

For he, the one I cannot content myself
Without – soon I saw him content himself without
me,
Hours when I am forgotten – (O weeks and months are
passing, but I
believe I am never to forget!)
Sullen and suffering hours – (I am ashamed – but
it is useless – *I am what I am;*)
WALT WHITMAN (1819-92)

But merely of two simple men I saw today on the pier
in the midst of the crowd, parting the parting of
dear friends,
The one to remain hung on the other's neck and
passionately kissed him,
While the one to depart tightly pressed the one
to remain in his arms.
WALT WHITMAN (1819-92)

Now of all that city I remember only the man who
wandered with me there, for love of me. Day by day, and
night by night, we were together. All else has long been

forgotten by me – I remember, I say, only one rude and ignorant man, who, when I departed, long and long held me by the hand with silent lips, sad and tremulous.

    WALT WHITMAN (1819-92)

Were are you, Pete? Oh! I'm feeling rather kinky – not at all peart, Pete – not at all.

    WALT WHITMAN (1819-92)
    regarding his friend, Peter Doyle

Yet each man kills the thing he loves,
    By each let this be heard,
Some do it with a bitter look,
    Some with a flattering word,
The coward does it with a kiss,
    The brave man with a sword.

    OSCAR WILDE (1854-1900)

And alien tears will fill for him
Pity's long-broken urn,
For his mourners will be outcast men,
And outcasts always mourn.

    OSCAR WILDE (1854-1900)
    epitaph on Oscar Wilde's tomb: lines from his *The*
      Ballad of Reading Gaol

I weep these three dead: You the most regretted; and he who responded with a touching love, the other who, without dying, deserted me, whose name sometimes comes back to me like a song.

    COMTE ROBERT DE MONTESQUIEU (1855-1921)

The disappearance of a strong father in childhood not infrequently favours the inversion [homosexuality].

SIGMUND FREUD (1856-1939)

He's lost him completely, as though he never existed.
Through fantasy, through hallucination,
he tries to find his lips in the lips of other young men,
he longs to feel his kind of love once more.

CONSTANTINE P. CAVAFY (1863-1933)

I killed Freda because I loved her, and she refused to marry me. I asked her three times to marry me, and at last she consented. We were to marry here and go to St Louis to live. I sent her an engagement ring and she wore it for a time. When she returned it I resolved to kill her. I would rather she were dead than separated from me living.

ALICE MITCHELL, 1892
American society girl/murderess
regarding her motive for murdering Freda Ward, 1892

I don't know how to say it … but … every time you say goodnight to me, and then go away, and shut the door of your room, I feel so terribly lost … I stare at your door through the darkness … I keep on staring and staring … and I long to get up … open your door, creep up to your bed, and kneel beside it. I want to take your hand, and – and tell you … but I know I mustn't, so I have to clutch hard to my bed – I grip it so tight that it hurts … Oh, I love you!

CHRISTA WINSLOE, 1932
German playwright
Manuela, in *Girls in Uniform*
to her schoolteacher Fräulein von Bernberg

There can be no relation more strange, more critical, than that between two beings who know each other only with their eyes, who meet daily, yes, even hourly, eye each other with a fixed regard, and yet by some whim or freak of convention feel constrained to act like strangers.

THOMAS MANN (1875-1955)
Narrator, in *Death in Venice*

He would not – and this was the test – pretend to care about women when the only sex that attracted him was his own. He loved men and always had loved them. He longed to embrace them and mingle his being with theirs. Now that the man who returned his love had been lost, he admitted this.

E.M. FORSTER (1879-1970)
Narrator, in *Maurice*

You will never succumb to the charms of any of your sex – What an arid garden the world must be for you.

VIRGINIA WOOLF (1882-1941)
letter to her sister, Vanessa Bell

I do not like to sleep at night, with your head against my shoulder; for I think of death, which comes so soon and enfolds us in too much sleep. I shall die, you will live: that is what keeps me awake. And yet aother fear: one day not to hear you breathing and your heart beating beside me.

JEAN COCTEAU (1889-1963)

Let our hearts break provided they break together.

C.S. LEWIS (1898-1963)

No, I'm not. But I soon will be.

TRUMAN CAPOTE (1924-84)

last words of Truman Capote when asked by friend Joanne Carson, 'Are you all right?'

How much of all this did I enjoy, this long pursuit of love through sex, out of which, in the end, I emerged as lonely as I began? ... Although so many boys had passed through my hands I lived with none of them, they came and went, ... at no point in this journey did I have a feeling of stability, of more than momentary satisfaction.

J.R. ACKERLEY, 1968

I'm scared to death of what's emerging in the gay middle class. I was at [the New York nightclub] the Saint in costume the other night and I was petrified. I felt like Jezebel when she came into the room with a scarlet dress. No one wanted to go near me. Everyone was so afraid to be different. I call it a gay middle-class vacuum. This conformity is a dangerous thing.

HIBISCUS, 1980s

We had an initiation ceremony – we'd all hold hands and we had ritualistic things that we said, something like, 'No gay person coming into the world will ever again have to feel alone and unwanted and rejected.'

HARRY HAY, 1980s

on the Mattachine Society, pioneer gay rights group

Someone perfectly alone as a gay person is not gay; he isn't acting as a gay, he isn't even having homosexual sex, except perhaps cautiously, the way many heterosexuals do.

He thinks that he is the only person who might be gay, and he probably wouldn't even be thinking *that* – since being the *only* one would mean that he is a monster – so he doesn't have any kind of social identity.

GUY HOCQUENGHEM, 1980s

It just isn't true that gay people are lonelier than ungay people (or whatever the opposite of gay is), and I'm in a position to know.

NED ROREM, 1982

[One] misconception is that fathers invariably reject their gay sons. In fact, it is often *the gay son who has rejected the father*.

CHARLES SILVERSTEIN, 1981

Fact: The Michigan Women's Music Festival announced that male children would not be allowed on festival grounds. Male children over the age of six were to be placed in a camp about ten miles away ... I refused to place my Jewish child in a camp because of his undesirability to Lesbian separatists.

SUSAN J. WOLFE, 1982

It's one thing to support Gay Rights. It's another to adore a man you know to be a homosexual, by which you make yourself miserable. By which you make him miserable. It's perverse.

BARBARA GRIZZUTI HARRISON, 1984

In 1970 I was 19, gay, and a medic with the Marines in Vietnam. The pain of seeing beautiful men I loved destroyed is still with me. These men stride through my dreams and fantasies. We must never allow another war to waste our brothers and sisters.

MIKE FELKER, 1984
former US Marine

How many lesbians are in nursing homes or other health-care facilities where they must conceal their identity and live out their lives as strangers in a strange land?

MONIKA KEHOE, 1986

Where are my hard-won ideas about separatism, confrontation, group consciousness? Are we not members of a lost and dispersed tribe, rather than errant offspring?

CARL WITTMAN, 1980s

While dressing today, I went to Barry's closet and, with a certain amount of relish, took a tie of his ... Tying the knot, I knew how handsome he thought me in it – perhaps how handsome I looked to him now, from some cloud – and I wept.

STEPHEN GREGO, 1987

Our community is experiencing the same kind of devastation that befell the survivors of the world wars. Nothing will alleviate our grief completely, because this tragedy is real and inescapable. But we don't have to cooperate or make it even worse by denying there's an epidemic and refusing to practise safer sex, fragmenting our community by blaming parts of it that we don't like for the disease, or becoming isolated and politically passive.

PAT CALIFIA, 1988

I spent the whole afternoon thinking about Marvin. I thought about why we were best friends and why I loved him so much. By the time I finished the piece, my grief had been replaced by a sense of resolution and completion ...

There's promise in a quilt. It's not a shroud or a tombstone. It's so important for people whose greatest enemy is despair. I really believe that the worst thing that could happen to us is to despair and to stop living and loving and fighting.

CLEVE JONES
founder of the NAMES Project, 1988
regarding the first quilt square designed for his friend,
Marvin Feldman

AIDS has come upon us with cruel abandon. It has forced us to confront and deal with the frailty of our being and the reality of death. It has forced us into a realization that we must cherish every moment of the glorious experience of this thing we call life. We are learning to value our own lives and the lives of our loved ones as if any moment may be the last.

ELIZABETH TAYLOR, 1988

I do hope it's acceptable for me to put the names of both my sons on a single panel. Sydney and Jim would have approved because they were close friends ...

I totally accepted the fact of their homosexuality. Unfortunately, the same cannot be said for their father, who is now my ex-husband.

Pray for all of us. I have two more gay sons, I live in fear.

JUDY SOONS, 1988

note submitted to NAMES Project with the panel honouring her two sons

Sexuality

Blessed is the man who knows how to make love
    as one wrestles in a gym,
and then goes home happy to sleep the day
    with a delicious young boy.
THEOGNIS
Greek poet, 6th century BC

I, for the sake of that Queen of love, like the wax of the
holy bees that is melted beneath the heat of the sun, waste
away when I look at the young limbs of blooming boys.
PINDAR (522 BC-443 BC)

Men who are slices of the male are followers of the male,
and show their masculinity throughout their boyhood by
the way they make friends with men, and the delight they
take in lying beside them and being taken in their arms.
And these are the most hopeful of the nation's youth, for
theirs is the most virile constitution …
    And so, when this boy-lover – or any lover, for that
matter – is fortunate enough to meet his other half, they are
both so intoxicated with affection, with friendship, and

with love, that they cannot bear to let each other out of sight for a single instant. It is such reunions as these that impel men to spend their lives together, although they may be hard put to say what they really want with one another; and indeed the purely sexual pleasures of their friendship could hardly account for the huge delight they take in one another's company.

PLATO (427? BC-347 BC)

Neglect your Guard, and let him get the best;
Then he'll be mild, then you a Kiss may seize,
He'll struggle, but at length comply with ease;
Reluctant, tho' at first you'll find him grow
Ev'n fond, when round your Neck his Arms he'll throw.

TIBULLUS (*c.* 60 and 48 BC-19 BC)

Although they have good-looking women, they pay very little attention to them, but are really crazy about having sex with men. They are accustomed to sleep on the ground on animal skins and roll around with male bedmates on both sides. Heedless of their own dignity, they abandon without a qualm the bloom of their bodies to others. And the most incredible thing is that they don't think this is shameful. But when they proposition someone, they consider it dishonourable if he doesn't accept the offer!

DIODORUS SICULUS
Roman historian, 20 BC
on homosexuality among Celtic males of the period

Count as three all those on a bed, of whom two are
active
And two are passive. I seem to relate a marvel,

174

Yet it is not a falsehood: the one in the middle
  performs doubly,
Pleasing in the back and being pleased in the front.
  STRATO, c. AD 2

Love is beautiful and decorous; pleasure is vulgar and
servile. For this reason it is considered uncouth for a free
man to be in love with slaves, since this sort of passion is
merely sexual, like relations with women.
  PLUTARCH (46?-120)

Men, leaving the natural use of the woman, burned in their
lust one toward another.
  THE BIBLE
  Romans 1:26

Thus I contaminated the spring of friendship with the dirt
of lust and darkened its brightness with the blackness of
desire.
  ST AUGUSTINE OF HIPPO (354-430)

A boy is for pleasure; a woman for children.
  PERSIAN PROVERB, 800

  'But humans should not be like birds or pigs:
  Humans have reason.
  Peasants, who may as well be called pigs –
  These are the only men who should resort to women.'
    MEDIEVAL POET, 1120?
    Ganymede, in *Ganymede and Helen*

You are the common desire of lasses and lads;
They sigh for you and hope for you because they know
    you are unique.
    HILARY THE ENGLISHMAN, 1150?

Venus kindles all fires, but the greatest heat
Is in sex with males; whoever has tried it knows it.
    MEDIEVAL MONK, 1150?

Alas, how can a love that's chaste
(Such as burns now so strongly within me),
Be seen by him whose love is otherwise?
    MICHELANGELO BUONARROTI (1475-1564)

Tell me, dearest, what is love?
'T is a lightning from above;
'T is an arrow, 't is a fire,
'T is a boy they call desire.
    FRANCIS BEAUMONT (1584-1616) AND JOHN FLETCHER
    (1579-1625)

I storm and I roar, and I fall in a rage,
And missing my Whore, I bugger my Page.
    JOHN WILMOT, EARL OF ROCHESTER (1647-80)

Buggery we chose and Buggery we allow
For none but fops alone to cunts will bow.
    JOHN WILMOT, EARL OF ROCHESTER (1647-80)

In England the vices in fashion are whoring and drinking,
in Turkey, Sodomy & smoking. We prefer a girl and a
bottle, they a pipe and a pathic – They are sensible people.
    LORD BYRON (1788-1824)

For boyish minions of unhallowed love
The shameless torch of wild desire is lit,
Caressed, preferred even to women's self above,
Whose forms for Nature's gentler errors fit
All frailties mote excuse save that which they commit.
LORD BYRON (1788-1824)

Erection: A word used only when speaking of monuments.
GUSTAVE FLAUBERT (1821-80)

Little you know the subtle electric fire that for
your sake is playing within me.
WALT WHITMAN (1819-92)

Tender, the young auburn woman,
By such innocence aroused,
Said to the blonde young girl
These words, in a soft low voice:

'Sap which mounts, and flowers which thrust,
Your childhood is a bower:
Let my fingers wander in the moss
Where glows the rosebud.'
PAUL VERLAINE (1844-96)

I spent the night between two fellows from the docks,
Who took turns, and cured me of the hots!
JEAN LORRAIN (1850-1906)

No civilized man ever regrets a pleasure, and no uncivilized
man ever knows what a pleasure is.
OSCAR WILDE (1854-1900)

Dark and wrinkled like a deep pink,
It breathes, humbly nestled among the moss
Still wet with love.
  PAUL VERLAINE (1844-96)
  'Sonnet to an Asshole'

The popular theory of the sexual instinct corresponds
closely to the poetic fable of dividing the person into two
halves – man and woman – who strive to become reunited
through love. It is, therefore, very surprising to find that
there are men for whom the sexual object is not woman but
man, and that there are women for whom it is not man but
women. Such *persons* are designated as contrary sexuals, or
better, inverts, and the situation of such a relationship is
called inversion. The number of such individuals is
considerable, although it is difficult to estimate them
accurately.
  SIGMUND FREUD (1856-1939)

I don't care what people do, as long as they don't do it in
the street and frighten the horses!
  MRS PATRICK CAMPBELL (1865-1940)
  when asked her opinion of homosexual affairs

They burned with each other, inwardly. This they would
never admit. They intended to keep their relationship a
casual free-and-easy friendship, they were not going to be
so unmanly and unnatural as to allow any heart-burning
between them. They had not the faintest belief in deep
relationship between men and men, and their disbelief

178

prevented any development of their powerful but suppressed friendliness.

D.H. LAWRENCE (1885-1930)
description of Gerald and Birkin, in *Women in Love*

Every farmer who has raised cattle knows ... that cows quite regularly mount cows.

ALFRED KINSEY (1894-1956)

Don't you know of same-gender heterosexual friendships in which there's a strong attraction? It doesn't have to be sexual to be romantic.

GEORGE CUKOR (1899-1983)

> I know women that don't like men
> The way they do is a crying sin.
> It's dirty but good, oh, yes, it's dirty but good
> There ain't much difference, it's just dirty but good.
> BESSIE SMITH (1894-1937)
> 'It's Dirty But Good'

Men who don't fall in love but just go for one-night stands and bar pickups, they get wolfish looking, you can see it in their eyes. Their eyes lose a certain ... humanity, because they only want the brutal sexual act.

TENNESSEE WILLIAMS (1912-83)

Seventy-five percent of our time at least is spent on lesbians.

WILLIAM MASTERS
sexologist

I just closed my eyes and thought of England.
> PETER FINCH (1916-77)
> regarding his controversial on-screen kiss with actor
> Murray Head in the film *Sunday, Bloody Sunday*,
> directed by John Schlesinger

'Liberace's Hot Nuts'
> LIBERACE (1919-87)
> inscription on glass nut bowls sold at the auction of
> his estate

The good thing about masturbation is that you don't have
to dress up for it.
> TRUMAN CAPOTE (1924-84)

> Your hand trembles in mine
> Like a frightened pigeon. I fear
> Your pink beak will peck
> My youth, the sole fruit I have.
> YUKIO MISHIMA (1925-70)

What the gay movement needs now is much more the art of
life than a science or scientific knowledge (or pseudoscien-
tific knowledge) of what sexuality is. Sexuality is a part of
our behaviour. It's a part of our world freedom ... Sex is not
a fatality; it is a possibility for creative life.
> MICHAEL FOUCAULT (1926-84)

I wish.
> HARVEY MILK (1930-78)
> American politician/activist
> comment made to Senator Briggs citing statistics that
> indicated that the average gay man has over five
> hundred sexual contacts

How many painful disillusions would be saved if, instead of thinking themselves obliged to say 'I love you', men would content themselves with saying 'I desire you'.

RENÉ GUYON, 1934

The Greek symbolizes ancient sex ... and homosexuality – uninhibited sexuality and wonderful bodies.

RAINER WERNER FASSBINDER (1946-82)

Sexual energy not used by homosexuals for procreation, as it is by heterosexuals, should be channelized elsewhere where its ends can be creativity.

HARRY HAY, 1951

The sailor who stands against a wall, looking down at the bobbing head of the gobbling queen, regards himself as master of the situation; yet it is the queen (does not that derisive epithet suggest primacy and dominion?) who has won the day, extracting from the flesh of the sailor his posterity, the one element in every man which is eternal (a scientific fact) and cellularly resembles not at all the rest of the body.

GORE VIDAL, 1968
Myra Breckinridge, in *Myra Breckinridge*

It's too bad that every male cannot have instruction from a female homosexual prior to marriage. Only a female homosexual really knows how to make love to a woman. We, as men, are kind of duds along those lines.

EARLE M. MARCH, 1972

The ass is the face of the soul of sex.
CHARLES BUKOWSKI, 1969

There will be sex after death, we just won't be able to feel it.
LILY TOMLIN, 1970s

What is the ultimate sexual rejection?
Having your hand fall asleep while you're masturbating.
JOKE, 1970s

Conventional heterosexual intercourse is like squirting jam into a doughnut.
GERMAINE GREER, 1970s

Bisexuality immediately doubles your chances for a date on Saturday night.
WOODY ALLEN, 1975

I don't think there's anything wrong with relating to people on the level of pure meat, as long as you don't get trapped into that all the time as a single level of consciousness – as some queens do.
ALLEN GINSBERG, 1975

Hey, don't knock masturbation. It's sex with someone I love.
WOODY ALLEN, 1977
Annie Hall

Bath sign language predates Noel Coward. The signals are the same throughout the world. Examples? If one's towel is knotted in the back, sodomy is the order of the night. Lying on one's back on a cot, legs ajar, is an open call for fellatio. and one doesn't have to be an Einstein to know what lying on one's stomach means.

ARTHUR BELL, 1977

There is no middle-class sexual style for men. What would it be based on? Golfing? Discussing stock options? Attending church? Downing highballs?

EDMUND WHITE, 1979

Voyeurism is a healthy, non-participatory sexual activity – the world *should* look at the world.

DESMOND MORRIS, 1974

Until more is known about the origins of heterosexuality it is difficult to believe that meaningful insights will be reached regarding the origins of homosexuality.

WILIAM MASTERS AND VIRGINIA JOHNSON, 1979

The idea of sex with a man doesn't turn me off, but I don't express it. I satisfied my curiosity about that years ago. I had lots of sex between the ages of three and four and the time I was fourteen or fifteen. Strange experiences with older boys. But men don't particularly turn me on. And, no, John [Oates] and I have never been lovers. He's not my type. Too short and dark.

DARYL HALL, 1980s

The big mistake that men make is that when they turn thirteen or fourteen and all of a sudden they've reached puberty, they believe that they like women. Actually, you're just horny. It doesn't mean you like women any more at twenty-one than you did at ten.

JULES FEIFFER, 1980

The cues that a woman receives from another woman are more subtle than the cues men give each other ... Two women do not have to explain away an erection should one of them get excited while they were having a tête-à-tête and talking about their sex lives.

PEPPER SCHWARTZ AND PHILIP BLUMSTEIN, 1973

Come forth, come forth, at least once every day!

JAMES BROUGHTON, 1982

Bringing guests home for sex is usually not advisable, even in a very open relationship. No matter how passionately two lovers pledge undying fidelity to one another, the unexpected presence of a third attractive body usually provides enough tinder to set off an emotional firestorm that makes the burning of Troy look like a quiet marshmallow roast.

BRYAN MONTE, 1986

In an enlightened culture to confine sex to procreative heterosexual monogamy is archaic.

PHIL NASH, 1986

Sexuality and self-esteem go together.

SARA CYTRON, 1988

Public sex is a problem that gay men are largely responsible for perpetuating and one that gay activists should not shunt. Besides the risk of arrest and danger of violence to those involved, public sex makes all gay men look bad in the eyes of the average American bigot. And, frankly, it's something that users of public facilities should not have to be exposed to – nor should their children.

DAVE WALTER, 1988

There'll be a group of four or five males, and it seems like one of them goes, 'Let's get Pointer!' And the other males start mounting him with erections … The males are constantly mounting each other.

RICHARD CONNOR, 1988
on dolphin behaviour

Watching safe-sex videos is like … watching professional football players touch. People don't want that.

PERRY ROSS
video merchandiser/officer of the Adult Video
Association, 1988

I'm scared to death of the individual who has no sexual desires, no romantic desires, no fantasies.

JOHN CARDINAL O'CONNOR, ROMAN CATHOLIC
ARCHBISHOP OF NEW YORK, 1988

The clone – the gay everyman – is vitally concerned with sexual expression.

JOHN PRESTON, 1983

Sex with strangers is an alternative to language, the code that replaces speech.

EDMUND WHITE, 1983